ƀ4

f

ELIZABETH RIGBY
LADY EASTLAKE

Elizabeth Eastlake from a painting
by Sir William Boxall, R.A.

MARION LOCHHEAD

Elizabeth Rigby
Lady Eastlake

JOHN MURRAY
ALBEMARLE STREET LONDON

Dedicated to
No. 50 Albemarle Street

Printed in Great Britain by
Cox & Wyman Ltd., London, Fakenham and Reading and
published by John Murray (Publishers) Ltd.

FOREWORD

Edinburgh
1961

My dear Sir John Murray,

In dedicating this book to your house, which Elizabeth Rigby knew so well and which, in a hundred and fifty years has become a person rather than a building, I should perhaps say a little about its writing. The idea was sown in my mind, although I did not then realise it, when I was engaged upon my Life of John Gibson Lockhart; for then I met Elizabeth Rigby as a friend of J. G. L., a contributor to his and your great-grandfather's *Quarterly Review*, and a woman of letters of considerable reputation and distinction. The woman who could be a pioneer in highbrow journalism, and could hold the respect, even the affection of the fastidious and difficult Lockhart, was worth discovering.

The clamour of two groups of Victorian children drove her from my mind, for a time; then, having escaped from nursery and schoolroom to the comparative peace of library and drawing-room, I found her again and enjoyed her conversation. To drop metaphor, I returned from social history to biography in a period already familiar and fascinating to me. I liked Miss Rigby, I continue to like her—on the whole, though somewhat shaken by the ferocity of her attack on the fellow-writer who least deserved it—Charlotte Brontë.

The material for this Life has not been abundant; the best source, her own Journals and Letters, the next her articles in *The Quarterly*. My heroine lacks, I know, the endless fascination and mystery of the Brontës, the brilliance of Jane Carlyle, the

v

profundity of George Eliot. She has, however, her own quality of mind, a vigour of personality that have made my time with her a stimulating period. If the result satisfies you and a reasonable number of other readers, I shall be happy.

Yours sincerely,
Marion Lochhead

ACKNOWLEDGEMENTS

I am grateful to Sir John Murray for giving me access to Lady Eastlake's unpublished letters and for the illustrations in this book; to Mrs. Osyth Leeston for much stimulating and constructive criticism of my MS; to Admiral Sir William James for his cordial permission to quote from his book, *The Order of Release;* and to Dr. William Beattie and his staff of The National Library of Scotland for their unfailing help.

CONTENTS

ILLUSTRATIONS

CHILDHOOD AND YOUTH
NORFOLK AND GERMANY

SIX years before Waterloo a girl was born in Norfolk that region of wide skies and lucid atmosphere, whose life was to have a spaciousness and freedom not granted to many Victorian women. Elizabeth Rigby may be called a pioneer of feminine journalism; a patroness of women of letters, as distinct from the poets and novelists; and, if not one of the great women travellers (for she cannot approach Isabella Bishop or Mary Kingsley) certainly a delightful writer of travel letters: altogether a woman who found her circumstances so wide that she need never demand any new freedom.

She was born in Norwich in 1809, fifth child and fourth daughter of Dr. Edward Rigby, an eminent physician and, at one time, Mayor of the city. He was something of a polymath: a good classical scholar, a keen naturalist, with a practical interest in agriculture.

In his own field of medicine he specialized in gynaecology and obstetrics of which he had ample experience at home. He was twice married and had fourteen children: two by his first wife, twelve by his second, Elizabeth's mother who was a Palgrave of Yarmouth. In 1817 this prolific and much enduring lady gave birth, at the age of forty, to four poor babes who, not liking this world overmuch, departed. Dr. Rigby was then seventy. His fellow-citizens presented him with a piece of plate; the *Morning Chronicle* celebrated the event in verse:

> Leda hatched four bantlings at a birth;
> Far greater praise, we must confess, is due,
> O most prolific Rigby, then to you.

His son Edward inherited his medical skill; his daughter Elizabeth may have owed something of her sense of literature to him. As a young man Dr. Rigby had travelled in France, on the eve of the Revolution. His letters home, describing the Fall of the Bastille and the end of the old régime, were carefully preserved, and published many years later by Elizabeth.

From her mother she inherited considerable strength of mind and character. Mrs. Rigby was clever and energetic, with a great deal of common sense, particularly in the bringing up of her children. Although she had so many she knew very well what to do: they were disciplined but not crushed; given much more freedom than most of their contemporaries, with plenty of outdoor life; never allowed to indulge in moods, nerves, or self-pity. In summer they moved to Framlingham where the children spent most of their time in the garden or fields or woods, 'playing every sort of game, climbing trees and haystacks, making fires in a dry ditch and roasting potatoes', according to Elizabeth's nephew who wrote a brief account of her.

It is a picture of childhood that seems to belong to the early twentieth rather than the early nineteenth century, to an era of blue serge or print frocks rather than to one of muslin; but the cult of primness and gentility had not begun, and Mrs. Rigby was not one to be ruled by a cult. Dress, too, was simple in style: little girls wearing high-waisted, narrow-skirted frocks with short sleeves, boys in long trousers with short jackets; there was none of the later Victorian elaboration. Probably the little Rigby girls wore serviceable prints and ginghams that washed easily and did not tear at a touch, and had their muslins kept for Sundays and parties.

The boys went to school, the girls had governesses with visiting masters for French, Italian and music. It was not, perhaps, very solid or methodical and in later years Elizabeth was to deplore 'a very deficient education'. Like many another clever girl of her own and of later generations, she was largely self-taught. She learned to read in the fullest sense of the term, and so acquired a key that opened many doors of learning. From implicit evidence in some of her *Quarterly* articles we may guess something of the mental background of her childhood; from her nephew's account we know that she had a normal little girl's fondness for dolls and a clever little girl's deftness in making their clothes and furniture. She loved books always, and from the age of eight took delight in drawing. It was to be a lifelong pleasure; literature was to be her vocation and career, but drawing her delight.

Dr. Rigby died in 1821 at the age of seventy-four. (His widow was to outlive him by more than fifty years, dying in 1872, within sight of her century.) After his death the family settled at Framlingham. There is no detail about their circumstances; only a surmise of comfort and security. There is no hint anywhere in Elizabeth's writing of any knowledge or memory of poverty, however genteel, of anxiety, even of awareness of money. A lady and her children could live in comfort and dignity, if not in grandeur, on a modest income, especially in the country or a country town, with pleasant society and country occupations.

Children in those days, and for at least a generation to come, had few books of their own, written for their own young selves. Elizabeth may have been thinking of her own childhood when she wrote in a review of juvenile books in 1842.

'Could the shade of a great-grandmother be recalled to earth, we can imagine no object in this age of wonders so likely to astonish her venerable mind as her little descendants' abundance of books. In her day, children were not looked upon as reading animals; the key of the little glass-fronted bookcase was as carefully kept from them as that of the sweetmeat cupboard'—but not in the Rigby household. There, the little glass-fronted bookcase, perhaps more than one, would be open to young readers of Maria Edgeworth's *Popular Tales, Parents' Assistant, Harry and Lucy,* and other volumes; the *Poems* of Jane and Ann Taylor, the *Hymns* of Dr. Watts; *Evenings at Home* by Mrs. Barbauld and Dr. Aiken; Mrs. Trimmer's famous *Story of the Robins* which, although intended to draw children from the vain fantasies of fairy-tale, is itself a delicious and formal fantasy of the nursery-life of birds.

Besides her beguiling *Robins*, Mrs. Trimmer, following the example of Mrs. Barbauld, had published many instructive little books of Lessons—in Scripture, in Ancient History, in Natural History. The influx of children's books was slowly but surely beginning.

There was a regrettable revolt against fairyland. Instruction lifted her warning voice and piety crept into the nursery, as part of the Evangelical movement. There was always, however, a little fantasy, a little fun and nonsense: Cowper had given the nursery (and library) in every well-appointed home *The Adventures of John Gilpin*. And it took more than evangelical vehemence or massive instruction to sweep away the old, beloved fairy tales. Children had too much sense to ignore or forget princesses and enchanters, magic beasts, youngest sons in search of a fortune and all that goodly company. The magic tales were still told and re-told by mother, grandmother or nurse; and there was now a translation from the elegant French of Monsieur Perrault, Madame d'Aulnoy and Madame Leprince de Beaumont of the courtly tales of French faery: *Beauty and the Beast, The Sleeping Beauty, Puss in Boots, Cinderella*.

Besides these, there were those grand romances and allegories that were never intended for children, but were calmly and rightly annexed by them: *Gulliver, Don Quixote, Robinson Crusoe, The Pilgrim's Progress*, which the mature Miss Rigby said 'could not be read too soon'. Her mature self recommended also *The Vicar of Wakefield* for children as for adults; realizing or remembering that half the delight of childish reading lies in discovering grown-up literature. A child who found such treasures was enriched for life. Behind some of the articles Miss Rigby wrote in the 1840's can be seen the happiness, freedom and mental health of her own childhood: a nursery and schoolroom ruled by wise and affectionate discipline with a respect for the freedom of a child's mind and personality.

This girlhood at Framlingham may have resembled that of Elinor, Marianne and Margaret Dashwood with their mother in their new cottage in Devonshire: not wealthy, luxurious or exciting, but comfortable, leisurely and cultivated: days filled with lessons at first, then with reading, music, drawing, walks and little diversions—a tea-drinking or a morning call where a light collation was served, or supper with talk, a little music, a game of cards. In the year of Elizabeth's birth Jane Austen moved to Chawton with her mother and sister, Parson Austen being dead; she was revising her *Elinor and Marianne* which would appear as *Sense and Sensibility*. Scott was at the full tide of creative genius, and the first Waverley Novels by The Great Unknown may well have found their way into the Framlingham household; his poems and Cowper's captivated Elizabeth as they did Marianne Dashwood. Her mother or one of her sisters may have read them aloud, as she sat drawing like Elinor.

This picture is imaginary but credible. The placid course of girlhood was broken by illness. Elizabeth doubtless outgrew her strength; she was five feet eleven. When she was convalescent, the family went, in 1827, to live in Germany, in Heidelberg for two years: an unusual venture for a middle-class family. The Grand Tour, interrupted by the war with France, had been resumed by the aristocracy, but the minor gentry, the professional and middle-class families travelled little beyond their own country.

Germany was less visited than France or Italy, and German was not yet a fashionable language, although its literature of the eighteenth century had strengthened the impact of the Romantic Revival. Girls in the schoolroom learned French and Italian.

The Germany of 1827 was a country of little kingdoms and dukedoms, of towns hardly changed in aspect since the Middle Ages, with gabled houses, steep roofs with a stork's nest, narrow cobbled streets, and beyond, a romantic landscape of woods and vineyards and castles above the river. The air was still heavy with the fragrance (or the vapours) of romanticism. Goethe was still living in Weimar with five more years of grand old manhood and poethood in prospect; the young Heine was in Munich, after his visit to England, and had made a name as poet with his first volume of lyrics, and as travel-writer with his *Harzreise*.

Germany meant music, poetry, learning; a new kind of art, a new way of life, another tradition; altogether a good tonic for a girl of unsatisfied mental appetite and intellectual energy. Elizabeth even in convalescence was too well-balanced to suffer from *Weltschmerz*, and Mrs. Rigby would not have permitted it to occur. This sojourn abroad was to her what college would be to girls of a later generation: an awakening, an enriching of the mind, a preparation for a career. She learned German thoroughly, studied the art and literature of the country, and in her subsequent work as journalist and reviewer, was to realize the practical value of such learning. Even in those uncrowded days it paid to specialize, to be equipped with some unusual accomplishment. Her first contribution to periodical literature was a story, in *Fraser's Magazine*, about the salt mines of Salzburg; and in 1830 she translated Waagen's book on *The Art Collections of England*.

On returning home, the Rigbys spent a year in London where Elizabeth settled down to a regular study of art, literature and music. She took drawing lessons, copied pictures in the National Gallery, attended concerts, read seriously and methodically. There is no Journal of that year as there is of her sojourn in Edinburgh a few years later, but from that Edinburgh record we know that she was a woman of the world as well as of letters; so may assume a certain amount of social life and diversion in London. Afterwards, they went to stay with Mrs. Rigby's family in Yarmouth; then to Framlingham again, and for a second visit to Germany.

Elizabeth wrote, for *The Foreign Quarterly Review,* an essay on Goethe, described as 'solid but unsympathetic'. In one of her articles in John Murray's *Quarterly Review,* in 1845, she discussed some *Biographies of German Ladies:* the Letters of Rahel Levin; the Correspondence of Bettina von Arnim with Goethe; the Life of Charlotte Streglitz. This may be quoted now, because in her criticism she drew upon her memories and impressions of German society in the 1830's, and the article is a record of this period. Her impressions were by no means favourable:

'We look to the biography and writings of a woman to show us the interior of a nation as well as of a family. Show us the occupations and opinions of the female half of a nation, and it is easy to predict the main features of the other half.' Her dislike of the ladies under review is apparent, and even now communicates itself to the reader:

'If we have laid down these books with greater pity, regret, and we may add disgust at the social structure of morals and religion now existing in Germany, it has been with less wonder at its formation—for which women were, indirectly, to blame.

'There is not, and perhaps never has been a nation arrived at the same degree of inward strength and civilization where the influence of women operates in so indirect and negative a way. . . . The German woman is feminine but nothing else; and herein lies the nullity of her influence in a social life.'

The German woman was emotionally unrestrained, her mind insufficiently developed to balance her sensibility; she erred 'not so much in the excess of devotion and self-abandonment as in the unrestrained indulgence of these impulses'. German youth was 'the most poetic in the world', but German middle-age was heavy, the ecstasy of romance followed by a 'selfish phlegm'. Feelings were the only guide to manners, and a poor guide they made; the manners were either uncontrolled or stiff. There could be no easy talk, no companionship between men and women, and this was disastrous for both.

'Man requires the resistance as well as the co-operation of the female partner in life'; and the woman who rejected her own intuitive wisdom in order to imitate man or submit herself to masculine judgement would 'involve herself in a web of illusion half sentimental, half sophistical' and would 'confirm men in their errors of pride and presumption, lack of fixed religion and

B

belief'. (The reader may wonder at times if Miss Rigby's impressions are of Germany in the 1830's or the 1930's!)

This lack shocked her. She had no use for the sentimental and intrusive piety that pervaded society in her youth; but religion must be the foundation and rule of life. Unlike most English critics she found German infidelity worse than French because it was so emotional, with 'every lawless thought, every idle dream, every dangerous imagination suffered to run their unhealthy race . . . piety professed without religion, and virtue without principle'.

Already aware of Europe, with her mental horizon wider than that of most of her female contemporaries in her own class, she was ready, in October 1838, for the journey that would lead her into literature.

The young Queen had just begun the adventure of her long reign. Many of her feminine subjects at this moment in the nursery or schoolroom, or secluded in domesticity, were destined for fame. The Brontës were at home in the parsonage at Haworth after their brief excursion into the world of school at Miss Wheeler's: Charlotte as teacher, Emily as pupil then teacher, Anne as pupil. Already they were living in their own vivid, visionary world; since childhood they had led this double life, and soon their dreams were to be transmuted into art—upon which Miss Rigby's views were to be vehemently expressed.

Marian Evans, who was of an age with the Queen, had finished her formal schooling, and was keeping house, happily and efficiently, for her widowed father at Griff in Warwickshire; educating herself in the classics and modern languages and in philosophy, with something like passion; absorbing, at the same time, the homeliness and sweetness of country life, all to be reflected in her novels.

Charlotte Yonge was still in the schoolroom, being prepared for confirmation, reading a great deal of history, solidly educated by her parents, and imagining, in her solitary walks round the garden, a series of families who would one day be created in fiction. Another girl was enduring a superficial and boring kind of schooling at a fashionable establishment in Brighton: Frances Power Cobbe, who was to follow Elizabeth on the path of journalism, though of a different kind from hers. Elizabeth's contemporary, the beautiful Mrs. Norton born a Sheridan, was winning fame for her poetry, and pluckily making a career for herself after the breakdown of her marriage. A group of future headmistresses and principals of women's colleges were enlarging, as far as they could, the restrictions of their education at home: Emily Davies, Anne Clough, Frances Buss, Dorothea Beale.

Closest, perhaps, in professional achievement though utterly opposed to her in opinions was the redoubtable Harriet Martineau: also a Norfolk woman. She was seven years older than Elizabeth, and by this time she was well-known as the author of didactic tales, written to illustrate her principles of political economy. She had travelled in America, met many eminent Americans, and made friends, most of whom she lost by her accounts of American life. In fact, she shared the unpopularity of Mrs. Tollope in this matter. As a Whig and a Unitarian she was unlikely to appeal to Miss Rigby, a good churchwoman and Tory, or to the orthodox and Tory *Quarterly*, and she had been severely castigated by Croker who was *The Quarterly's* executioner in chief. This did not wound her. On the contrary she declared that such condemnation was better publicity for her than the praise of the Whiggish *Edinburgh Review*. But that may have been a whimsical insistence that bitter pills were really sweet grapes.

Altogether the feminine world was far from somnolent, and any listener with ear to the ground might well have heard the march of the vanguard of great Victorian women. At the moment, there was a great deal of excitement and gossip about the girl Queen: her appearance, her habits, her court, her coronation, her possible marriage. There had not been a reigning Queen since Anne, about whom no one could be excited. Most people looked forward to a long, glorious and virtuous reign. There was some cynicism, however, with a little mockery of the plump little Majesty with her imperious ways and artless chatter; on the whole, sympathy and hope.

Women were by no means fragile, helpless or secluded, inert in body or in mind. All the same, for an unmarried lady, even of a discreet age, to set forth to the little known shores of the Baltic, even on an entirely proper visit to a married sister, was indeed an adventure, and literally something to write home about.

LETTERS FROM THE BALTIC

IN October 1838 Elizabeth began her complicated journey to Reval in the Baltic Provinces of Russia, where a married sister had her home. From a letter to John Murray written a few years later, it appears that there were two sisters in the province; and from the day of her departure from England Elizabeth wrote long letters to her mother, which were afterwards adjusted and trimmed into a book.

'Of all the modern pleasures and luxuries which the blessings of peace have brought in their train, none are more universally desired, pursued, attained and abused than those of travelling'— so she began her narrative. She was no novice in travel; but the Baltic was an unknown sea to most Englishwomen, Russia an unknown and barbarous country. Elizabeth set out well equipped with courage, resourcefulness, humour and a lively interest in new people and new scenes.

In her first letter, her fellow-travellers are lightly but clearly sketched: an old French officer, very courteous and 'unobtrusively attentive to others'; an English gentleman 'with a high priestral air and aristocratic bearing'—the new type of milord, more solemn that the old; a very old Swedish lady who might be 'a worthy woman' but 'lacked the good taste to seem so' for 'it would be difficult to define to what school of propriety' her manners belonged if to any. 'May Neptune not spare her,' added Miss Rigby with a sad lack of charity and of foresight; for Neptune spared none of the company, not a honeymoon couple who found Cupid 'anything but a good sailor', and not even Miss Rigby herself. There were three blank and dreadful days of sea-sickness and fear of shipwreck. A girl among the passengers felt that at such a crisis she ought to pray for her enemies, but could think of none, until she recalled the directors of the shipping company who had sent forth so unseaworthy a vessel; so she prayed for them, to her own spiritual comfort and possibly to their advantage. The ship was too heavily laden for safety, with a cargo of lead which submerged the foredecks and lifted the aft-deck out of the water; with other cargo in every available space, and a wretched horse on deck, in an open crib, which died of its sufferings.

They put into Christiansand in Norway, a blessed relief; sailed on to Copenhagen, past Hamlet's Castle of Krönborg and Elsinore 'that key that unlocks the narrow sluice-gates of the Baltic'. There, with a pilot on board, their captain had a little leisure for conversation, and entertained his passengers with re-miniscences of Nelson. Like Nelson he was a Norfolk man, and in his youth had served under the great little admiral for whom he had a true sailor's hero-worship. He had also a romantic devotion, not shared by his female listeners, for Lady Hamilton—'Nelson's evil angel under the most bewitching of female forms' in Miss Rigby's eyes. She had lived on board and had captivated all the young officers 'as much by her intercession in cases of petty delinquency as by her irresistible fascination of personality and manners'.

It was fascinating talk; treasure for any novelist, and 'so many of the present day have launched their literary barks upon the waves'. The captain was pronounced another Marryat.

Copenhagen was delightful. No doubt any haven would have been heaven after those stormy seas, but the little city sur-rounded by woods and meadows was enchanting in itself:

'There is something very pleasant in entering an entirely new place where you neither take nor leave a character,' admitted this decorous lady, with some relish in her freedom; 'where you may stare about you, look behind you, and in short dispense with all those little decorums which you have the distinct recollection of having learnt with exceeding repugnance during your child-hood.'

She, and some of her fellow-passengers, had letters of introduction to a Danish gentleman who acted as guide, with more zeal and courtesy than linguistic ability. Knowing a little of many languages he had the idea of mixing them all well together instead of concentrating upon one.

'Our conversation was therefore highly polyglotic', highly diverting and even frivolous: 'We wandered through the streets, a very merry group, till nightfall recalled us to the ship.' Next day was spent in pleasant *tourisme*, and in buying souvenirs in the shape of toys and wood carvings; then they sailed on to Kronstadt.

Here they found the complication of the Russian calendar: 'double dates and other strange and double-faced things', including the ways of the Customs and 'the intimate understanding which exists between Russian justice and Russian roubles, by virtue of which the former always abdicates to the latter'. Transferring into a small steamboat, Elizabeth proceeded to St. Petersburg, 'sailing apparently upon the bosom of the ocean into a city of palaces'.

There they were boarded by the Customs whose officers 'proceeded to turn out the gentlemen's pockets and the ladies' reticules' which appeared to Elizabeth to be 'a most admirable training for pickpockets'. A further inspection on land meant the opening of boxes, scattering of garments and other possessions. culminating in 'the devastation of an English writing-case' in which the searchers 'soiled the writing-paper and spilt the ink, mixed up wax, wafers and water-colours' and 'shook out the blotting-book' in a search for contraband Russian banknotes, They 'scattered abroad letters of introductions, cards of address, and other papers, ransacked the private drawer, and displaced all the steel paraphernalia' on which, to the joy of the owner, they cut their fingers.

But all things come to an end, and at last the weary and irate travellers were allowed to the English boarding-house, kept by Mrs. Wilson on the English Quay: a 'well-conducted and most respectable establishment' much frequented not only by the English but by those travelled Russians who found there some reflection of the comfort they had enjoyed in England.

St. Petersburg was strange and fascinating, a city of the Orient amid snow and chill waters, with mosque-like churches having star-painted domes and spires that soared above the low buildings around them 'blazing like flaming swords in the cold rays of a Russian October setting sun'.

A letter of introduction brought a Baron S. to call upon Miss Rigby; he was an aide-de-camp to the Emperor, and fort-major of the city: 'a pale young man' in a gorgeous uniform, with manners of a heart-warming simplicity and kindness. He provided her with a soldier as bodyguard, as casually, so she reported, as he might have offered her a pair of shoes. The soldier acted also as messenger, and in spite of the barrier of language was most helpful. The Baron himself took Elizabeth driving through the city. She loved sightseeing, and wrote a long account of the churches and museums with their incredible treasures. The Baron was almost too conscientious a cicerone:

'With military precision he parcels Petersburg out into districts, lays his plans of attack overnight' all for the benefit of 'a most thankless recruit'. Elizabeth would have preferred to stand and stare, to sit and think, or merely to sit a little more. She managed to arrange a compromise: after a dutiful and strenuous morning of sightseeing she enjoyed 'a graceless stroll' by herself on the Nevsky Prospekt, and there discovered the human pageant which delighted her: the coachman of a droshky; a peasant—'by birth a serf, and in gait a prince' wrapped in sheepskin with a multi-coloured belt, looking like 'the living effigy of an old patriarch'. The scriptural and oriental aspect of the city struck her more and more. It was a varied pageant—Finns, Tartars, Circassians, all in native costume—yet it was somehow not gay. There were too few comfortable pedestrians, 'that mainspring of gaiety in other cities', and fewer women. The Court and society had not yet returned for the winter.

On Sunday she went to the English Church where the congregation was chiefly of English merchants and their families, most of them descended from Englishmen settled a century or more ago in St. Petersburg. They formed a separate and very distinct community with their own tradition and way of life; many of them of aristocratic birth, sons and grandsons of cadets of great families who had gone out into the world to seek their fortune. They were among the most loyal subjects of the Emperor, but they kept apart; and they maintained the best English traditions and standards of punctuality, probity in business, utter integrity and a great practical charity:

'Nowhere can England be seen to better advantage than in the person of the British Factory'—as this community was called.

The Baron took her to the wedding of a pretty girl to an aged bridegroom. Elizabeth looked on benignly, with pity for the bride and a keen interest in the ceremonial details: the exchange of rings, the crowning of bride and groom, their receiving of Holy Communion. It was all very picturesque, but she found the bridgeroom a little absurd in his 'stupendous headgear' with a candle in his hand.

At the warm invitation of the Baron and his wife, Elizabeth presently moved, somewhat reluctantly, from the boarding-house with its 'few thin ghosts of English comfort' to the Baron's own home. There she was offered a choice of eight rooms, but was somewhat disconcerted by finding that none of them was a spare bedroom; she might have her hosts' bedroom or the children's; or the drawing-room, the study or the dining-room. Having chosen this last as farthest from the nursery, she found 'an ample corner partitioned off by a screen, and all my things arranged in order'; and there enjoyed sound sleep.

One of her last inspections was of the prison of which her host was governor. The prisoners were of every race within the Empire. Murderers, an Arab prince among them, were chained hand and foot, but otherwise, conditions were not so horrifying as she had feared. The prisoners were all together in one large room which was kept clean, bright and aired; there were wash-basins for the cleansing of their bodies and a great ikon with an ever-burning lamp, for the comfort of their souls.

Her journey to Reval, fixed for the end of October, had to be postponed; she went down with fever—'a kind of invisible *douane* in the air' to which most English travellers had to submit. It was not until late November that she set forth, in a *calèche* drawn by four horses, along the snowy roads that were not yet hard enough for a sledge. Her friends had revised her wardrobe: her English straw hat was exchanged for a quilted silk cap edged with fur; her fur-lined cloak and other wraps 'held up to derision as mere cobwebs against the cold'; finally, with a fox fur drawn over innumerable garments, 'as many as one might expect to wear in a lifetime', she drove off through the wide, white landscape.

At the first post-house she was surrounded by a fascinated crowd who gazed on her as on a living exhibit, and put her through a detailed catechism; then the hostess gave the audience a twopence coloured version, subtracting years from the traveller's age, adding roubles to her fortune, elevating her to the nobility. Elizabeth now began to prove the truth of her own earlier reflection:

'An inherent talent for sightseeing is a blessing not sufficiently to be prized, one equally commendable in its exercise as in its reward. It involves many Christian virtues, and a large share of corporeal strength. It requires its possessor to be meek, long-suffering and believing; to be patient when he feels no interest, to deny himself when he does'. She decided that 'sightseeing in drops is a cordial, in draughts a poison'.

Upon entering Estonia she was at first within sight and sound of the sea, then drove across a wide plain bordered by forests where the wolves howled, and sometimes came close. It was so cold that the sherry in her travelling-flask was frozen. Another night was spent in a post-house, and next day 'late, late in the gloaming' like Kilmeny she came home; for it was home, to be with this dear sister—'a joy too much for the poor heart to hold' at first, and 'a blissful agony'. The joy became cosy and domestic, as she began to be absorbed into this strange yet dear household, to make the acquaintance of her nieces and nephews 'those small and unread editions of a dear and familiar type', and to have long, intimate talks with her sister.

Soon after her arrival, the family left Reval for the country, for a great house splendidly furnished, if somewhat lacking in English comfort. But by this time the traveller was adapted to new ways. She could even accept the un-English breakfast 'which here is not considered a meal, and not half the respect paid to it which the simplest lunch-tray would command with us'—a mere trifle of coffee and bread and butter, taken anywhere—in one's own room, in the study or the dining-room, or, by the children, while running up and down and round the house: crumbs and buttery smears were apparently not frowned upon. The real or second breakfast (luncheon in the English sense) was a formal and substantial meal, beginning with *hors-d'œuvres*, continuing with soup or with *Brei*—a kind of porridge served with cream—and with a succession of rich dishes. The service was *à la Russe* as it was called in England, and as Elizabeth had seen it in Germany: the meat carved at a side-table and handed round, followed by the vegetables and sauces. In England the old fashion lingered of having everything on the table, not served separately course by course, the roasts, joints and fowls carved by host or hostess. This new way was not altogether commended; the vegetables were brought so long after the meat that this had either grown cold or been already eaten. Tea at six o'clock was simply tea, of the finest quality, relished like wine; supper, like the breakfast-luncheon, was an enormous meal.

Housekeeping in Estonia was a serious business. In England the good housewife had a well-stored larder, perhaps also a still-room; but there were shops at hand; even in the country, there was a neighbouring market town. Here, in the depths of the country amid snowy plains and forests, the house must be provisioned as for a siege. The storeroom was 'a very warehouse' stocked with rolls of linen, bundles of flax, hanks of wool, balls of twine, stacks of candles; with chests of flour, salt, sugar and sago; drawers full of dried fruit, quantities of herbs and spices; flagons of spirits and liqueurs, a supply of home-made medicines. Liquor was brewed in the house, soap and candles were made. House-keeping—*Wirtschaft*—was a major and honourable craft: 'The very word possesses a talismanic power' especially over girls pre-paring for marriage and for brides. It was very much what an English household had been in the country, a century earlier.

In the great servants' hall or people's room, *Volkstube*—which was 'a room for an artist' with its black, earthen floor, its walls of variegated black, red and yellow, its huge terracotta stove and wooden benches—the maids sat spinning; some of them bare-foot, all of them in peasant dress of striped petticoat and blue or grey jacket, their hair loose about their shoulders. Most of them were pretty though few of them were clean: 'But every vice has its pleasant side, and the worst of dirt and filth is that they are so picturesque.' Some of the flax thus spun was woven in the cot-tages on the estate; the finer linen was the work of a master weaver who went from one mansion to another with his book of patterns.

On Twelfth Day (by the English calendar) the family paid a visit to a neighbouring estate. Again Elizabeth horrified her hosts by her notions of travelling dress—especially her silk stockings and satin slippers! The maids promptly shod her in red woollen socks and fur boots, and she sank into a bed of cushions topped by a bearskin cover, and so made the journey unfrozen.

At dinner, the ladies sat on one side of the table, the men on the other, neither sex paying much attention to the opposite. They dined on roast elk which resembled venison, on a preserve of rose leaves—'a luscious kind of ambrosia, like eating perfume' —and finally on a walnut ice, delicious in the hot room: al-together a fairy-tale kind of banquet. After dinner the ladies again sat by themselves, gossiping, playing bagatelle, making music; the men withdrew to smoke and play cards until supper.

Having seen so much of life in a great house, Elizabeth wished to see that of a cottage, and was taken to one, built of logs, with a double wall at the entrance: the space between the walls occupied by a litter of pigs 'and some other little animals' who were found, on inspection, to be children. The interior was dark and smoky, the big room dominated by the stove which was fireplace and furniture in one; the children climbed up and down its shelves, and a baby lay asleep on the top ledge. A horse, cows and hens shared the place with their owners. A Scot might have said 'the clartier the cosier', but Elizabeth did not appear to find it 'clarty' or dirty: there was 'nothing in all this to disgust'. She admired the healthy children, and gave them the rare treat of some rolls of white bread.

The village church was Lutheran, not Orthodox, and was unimpressive except for the devout attention of the congregation of poor folk. Elizabeth wrote a long account of Lutheranism and its functioning, adding with reason: 'You must tire of my lamentable Church history.'

Early in the new year the family returned to Reval: a formidable undertaking for 'the hayloft, the cellar, the larder and the dairy' had all to be transported. A succession of carts went first; the *Herrschaft* followed. The children were dressed in layers of garments, topped by a quilted pelisse, until 'within the case of clothes before you which stands like a roll-pudding tied up ready for the boiler, no one would suspect the slender, skipping sprite that your little finger can lift with ease'.

The little head was tied up in a handkerchief binding cheeks and chin, like a nun's wimple; a wadded hat was set on top, draped with veils 'through which the brightest little pair of eyes in the world faintly twinkled like stars through a mist'. Finally this bundle was picked up by a servant and carried to the sledge; which to well-brought-up female readers may recall John Humphreys in *The Wide, Wide World* picking up Ellen

Montgomery when she came shuffling out of Alice's room in borrowed shawls and moccasins, with a green veil over her bonnet.

Town life was formal and fashionable, with morning calls, dinner parties (at two o'clock), evening receptions; always with a virtual segregation of women from men, the former longing to dance, the latter absorbed in cards. Estonian social conventions were over-strict to an English mind; one hears the echo of a sigh of boredom behind the lively description; there was so little good talk, so little ease of manner.

Elizabeth began a new study. 'The best souvenir the traveller can carry away of a foreign country, better than journal or sketch-book, is a knowledge of the language'. Already equipped with two of these, she prepared to add the third. She practised her Russian upon her maid, 'I sit and clip the Emperor's Russian without the slightest remorse',. while Sascha 'either *coiffé's* or *decoiffé's*' her mistress. The way of learning was long and hard and there were many lapses; the grammar was 'excessively verbose and intricate', the declensions complicated, and 'the quantities of proverbs, formal phrases and orientalisms' added to the difficulties. Elizabeth persevered, without much apparent reward in literature; the great novelists of the century, Tolstoi, Dostoievsky and Turgenev were still in their boyhood or youth. Cultivated Russians read chiefly translations of English, French and German novels. Maria Edgeworth's *Helen* was popular.

The coming of spring was a revolution and a revelation. Sledges, furs, double windows disappeared. It was not, however, altogether lovely. The streets were still slippery, and Elizabeth and her sister, walking to a friend's house two doors away, slipped and slid down a long slope of glass; they rose, but could move neither forwards nor backwards until a kindly, rough-shod sailor hauled them to safety. In the country it was delicious, with all things growing, with new life in the sweet air and running water.

The advancing year brought further exploration of countryside and seaports, more outdoor pleasures: a fair, a picnic, and a family gathering at a great house. This was not 'one of those rude, indecorous gatherings' known in England, but 'an orderly meeting of courteous individuals' whose kinship did not lessen their formality. Estonian etiquette was precise and stiff; the English guest found her hosts 'like the translated souls of my great-grandfathers and grandmothers.' Little girls were dressed and expected to behave like miniature women; Elizabeth, recalling the happy freedom of her own childhood, pitied them and longed to see an untidy English child.

Another winter was spent in St. Petersburg. The patriarchal way of life fascinated her; the family was more than the group of parents and children and near kin; it included the servants; and a regiment was a military family. On feast days the lady of the house would kiss her servants, a general kiss his men, the Emperor kiss his officers. The kiss was 'rather a greeting than a caress' and came 'equally from religious feeling and from oriental custom'.

The presence of the Court made this winter a brilliant season of functions and pageants. It was a far cry from the small pleasures of a country town, but Elizabeth sailed placidly through all the splendours and grandeurs as no doubt she did through the tea and supper parties at home. Her artist's eye was delighted by the Court costumes, unchanged through the centuries: the dress of white satin embroidered with gold, the robes of red or green velvet also worked in gold, the high fan-shaped headdress with its long veil; all very Eastern and gorgeous; the marvellous display of jewels, chiefly of diamonds.

The formality was broken at the masked balls which indeed gave to Elizabeth's mind, more freedom than was decorous. The gaieties culminated at the carnival, in Butter Week, when all the butter should be eaten before the long, strict fast of Lent; and with Lent came her departure from Russia. She left the country which had so fascinated her 'with the highest faith in its destiny, but also the reluctant conviction that at this present time Russia is the country where the learned man wastes his time, the patriot breaks his heart, and the rogue prospers'. That was Russia of 1840.

In 1841 her letters of travel were published, anonymously, by John Murray, under the title: *A Residence on the Shores of the Baltic Told in Letters.* For the copyright she was paid £100. The book was extremely popular, and a second edition was brought out as *Letters From the Shores of the Baltic.*

For an early Victorian lady brought up for the most part in provincial seclusion, it had been a considerable adventure. Other Victorian ladies were to be more daring, run very great risks— Isabella Bishop and Mary Kingsley among them. About this time, the Honourable Emily Eden was staying with her brother, the Governor-General of India, observing and recording many curious and exotic things. Her Letters too would prove delightful. But in 1841 the woman traveller who could talk easily and vividly on paper, who could record details of feminine and domestic interest, and captivate the common reader, was a rare, possibly a new figure, in literature.

It is small wonder that Miss Rigby found herself, if not so suddenly and resoundingly famous as Byron, certainly in decided favour with her public, and with her publisher John Murray, the second of his line, 'the Anak of publishers' in Byron's phrase, known in his circle as the Emperor.

III

'JOHN MURRAY STREET'

THE House of Murray had been founded by the Emperor's father, John the First: a London Scot, born MacMurray but dropping the Mac for simplification. A retired officer of the Royal Marines he bought the bookselling business of one William Sandby in Fleet Street, and enlarged it into a small publishing house. One of his books was Isaac D'Israeli's *Curiosities of Literature*, others were Mitford's *History of Greece* and the *Memoirs* of Lord Lovat; he also brought out a new edition of *The Castle of Otranto*.

John the Second, born in 1778, greatly developed the business. He published poetry, *belles lettres*, travel and cookery books, ranging from Byron to Mrs. Rundell, that admirable predecessor of Mrs. Beeton. In 1809 he founded *The Quarterly Reveiw* with William Gifford as editor, and a good team of scholars and men of letters. Sir Walter Scott contributed to the first number and to many a later one, writing a review of *Burns's Reliques . . . Letters and Poems*, and one of Southey's translations of *The Chronicles of the Cid*. In 1812 Murray moved to 50 Albemarle Street which became both home and publishing house. In the drawing-room there he used to receive his authors and contributors to *The Quarterly*. In that room Scott and Byron met, one day in 1815, with great mutual liking and sympathy. Together they limped downstairs, watched by a small boy, John Murray the Third, who reflected that he had never before seen two lame men walk downstairs together. This boy grew up to become the warm friend of Elizabeth Rigby—at this time a small girl in Norwich.

The famous room at No. 50 was at once drawing-room, library, office, club and centre of literary affairs. Here, after long discussion, a little group—Murray and Thomas Moore among them—sadly decided to burn Byron's Journals, compelled by the attitude of the formidable Lady Byron.

Charles Lamb declared that the street should be called 'John Murray Street'. Mrs. Somerville remembered that 'no house in London was more hospitable and agreeable' and that John Murray's dinners were brilliant, himself 'gentlemanly, full of information, and kept up the conversation with spirit'. The men of letters of the later Regency, of George IV's reign and William's, and Victoria's first decades, gathered here. Scott visited the house when he came to London, and his brilliant son-in-law John Gibson Lockhart came, not only as guest but as one of the house, for in 1826 he became editor of *The Quarterly Review*.

No publisher is without troubles, and the Anak had his share. Mrs. Rundell was a best seller, but she was exacting. She was one of the pioneers in the literature of cookery, preceded only by Mrs. Cleland and Mrs. Glasse. The housewife of the eighteenth and early nineteenth centuries had, as a rule, her private 'receipt book', but there was a need for a compendium, available to all, of recipes and instructions. Cookery was elaborate, the lady of the house must be able to plan and order a dinner of many courses, to instruct a new cook if necessary, even, in an emergency, to cook dinner herself. Mrs. Rundell assembled a large number of recipes, from soups to sweets and savouries, including preserves and still-room cookery; she gave clear instructions about buying as well as about cooking food, and was altogether a Housewife's Companion.

'Egad, one wonders that there should be any bad dinners going' was the comment of one masculine admirer. The first edition of the work was quickly sold; a second was revised and enlarged and given illustrations and diagrams. Then the ungrateful author tried to transfer the rights to Longman. Murray took legal action and acquired full publication rights for £2000. Thomas Moore remarked that Milton had been paid £5 for *Paradise Lost*. The book continued to sell and to repay its publisher.

His various ventures prospered. In 1828 he began the famous series of guide books with a volume of *Travels on the Continent*, following it with a *Guide for Travellers on the Continent* with maps. In 1824 he took over from Constable their unsuccessful *Mrs. Markham's History of England* which forthwith sold in large numbers. Mrs. Markham was in real life Mrs. Penrose, wife of a clergyman, and she had written the book for her own children. It taught history in dialogue between a mother and her three children, Richard, George and Mary, mamma relating the incidents and answering questions. Almost equally successful was *Little Arthur's History of England* by Maria Graham, afterwards Lady Callcott. Mrs. Markham, at Richard's request, further produced a *History of France*; and these three volumes remained classics of the schoolroom almost till the end of the century.

Meanwhile *The Quarterly* flourished, in spite, or perhaps because of a savagery of reviewing almost incredible today. It was in *The Quarterly* that John Wilson Croker wrote his famous and infamous attack on Keats, while in the sister magazine across the Border, in *Blackwood's*, John Gibson Lockhart dealt the dying poet another blow. Lockhart, brilliant, proud, and at this time almost uncontrollable in his satiric passion, had been introduced to Isaac D'Israeli in 1819 by William Blackwood as 'a very uncommon young man'. He was an advocate at the Scottish Bar, after a brilliant career in classics at Glasgow University and at Oxford. In 1820 he made his happy marriage with Scott's elder daughter Sophia. In his career at the Bar he was sound but not notable; his vocation was to journalism, then a new career for a scholar and gentleman, and in 1825 D'Israeli recommended him to Murray as editor of *The Quarterly*. Gifford had retired in 1823, and his successor J. T. Coleridge had not been able to hold office for long, because of his legal duties.

'The more I think of this affair,' wrote D'Israeli, 'the more I am quite overcome by what he has already achieved; never did the finest season of blossoming promise a richer gathering'.

It was an alluring prospect for a young man of ambition—

Lockhart had just entered his thirties—but Scott his chief and best counsellor was not altogether approving. Journalism was not entirely well-seen as a profession. Scott the Sheriff had the law as well as literature in his bones, and spoke of authorship as a good stick but a bad crutch for a man to lean upon.

'It is very true that this department of literature may and ought to be rendered more respectable than it is at present, but I think this is a reformation more to be wished than hoped for, and should think it rash for any young man of whatever talent, to sacrifice, nominally at least, a considerable portion of his respectability in Society'—he wrote to Murray, who reassured him.

The appointment was one which 'I verily believe is coveted by many of the highest literary characters in the country' and, far from diminishing his respectability, would 'entitle its possessor to enter into and mix with the highest classes of society'. The salary 'without writing a line, and merely for performing the duties of an editor' would be £1,000 which Lockhart's own contributions could easily bring up to £1,500—'and take no serious portion of his time either'. So, in January 1826, Lockhart brought Sophia and their little son Johnny to London to begin a career that ended only two years before his death. He is one of the great editors, as well as the great biographers of literary history. A complex and difficult character, deeply reserved, he felt and inspired a profound affection and loyalty in those who saw beneath the surface; his friends were true, and most of his contributors became his friends. He was settling himself firmly in the saddle for his long ride, when young Miss Rigby went to Heidelberg.

Both Murray and Lockhart were sympathetic with new ventures. They might almost be called feminists, for many of the women writers of the 1830's and 1840's were published from Albemarle Street. Miss Rigby had some distinguished elder sisters in that household, Fanny Kemble the actress among them. Murray published her play, *Francis the First*, and her *Journal From*

America. This was not well received, even by *The Quarterly,* where Croker deplored its bad taste. *The Athenaeum* called it 'this very lamentable Journal'. All the same, it found admiring readers who enjoyed its liveliness; among them Lady Callcott, whom no one could accuse of vulgarity. Another was Sir Francis Head, the author and traveller, who protested against the new gentility:

'People say she is vulgar! So was Eve, for she scratched whatever part of her itched, and did a hundred things which we would call vulgar. But the fact is that everything is vulgar nowadays' (1835), and 'poor Fanny Kemble has fallen a victim to this tyranny. Her book is full of cleverness, talent, simple-heartedness and nakedness'.

On a higher plane was Mrs. Somerville, the quiet little Scotswoman who became one of the finest mathematicians and scholars of her day, whose name was to be given, more than a generation later, to one of the new colleges for women. In 1831 Murray published her *Mechanism of the Heavens,* printing 750 copies which were all sold. The author was to have had two-thirds of the profits, but he gave her the whole:

'I am over-paid by the honour of being the publisher of so extraordinary a person' he wrote to her; and he continued to publish her scientific works.

Mrs. Somerville was, in her gentle way, a most charming and feminine woman; but more dazzling of allure was Mrs. Norton, Irish by birth and a Sheridan, beautiful, witty and unhappy. Her long poem *The Voice From the Factories*—perhaps the first poem with a purpose to achieve popularity—appeared in 1836, and shares with the legislation of Lord Shaftesbury the honour of awakening the public conscience about child labour and conditions in factories.

An article in *The Quarterly* on 'Modern English poetesses' called her 'the Byron of modern poetesses' which was, in Victorian slang, coming it a bit strong. Some of her fellow poetesses were harshly treated, and she wrote, in relief and gratitude, to the

Emperor that 'poisoned daggers are a joke to being laughed at in *The Quarterly*'.

She enjoyed a mild flirtation with her publisher, was a frequent guest at his house, and in *The English Bijou Almanac* of 1842 thus addressed him:

> *John Murray! Dare I call thee John?*
> *Yes; for who calls thee Mister Murray?*
> *The first familiar name's the one*
> *That puts us authors in a flurry;*
> *The first familiar name is that*
> *Long linked with memories bright and pleasant*
> *With hours of intellectual chat*
> *O'er claret, venison, grouse and pheasant;*
> *And all the sunshine, clouds and blame*
> *That hang round Byron's chequered story,*
> *Whom thy discernment led to fame,*
> *When fools denied the wreath of glory.*

Another lady, less gifted, was also less amiable. Mrs. Jameson, famous and popular in her day as art critic and historian, expected him to publish her *Guide to the Picture Galleries in London* without seeing the MS. To this he replied firmly and reasonably:

'My rule is never to engage in the publication of any work of which I have not been allowed to form a judgement of its merits and chances of success, by having the MS left with me a reasonable time. . . . As you expect money from the work which you wish to allow me the honour of publishing, how am I to judge of its value if I am not previously allowed to read it?'

She capitulated.

The firm was expanding; the boy who had watched the two lame geniuses limp downstairs together had grown to manhood, and was ready to share the affairs of state:

'Pray encourage him to proceed,' Lockhart wrote to John the Second—being himself of an age between father and son. 'His

youth, his different circle of acquaintances, his own selected pur-
suits are all new sources on which we may hope to draw largely
for spirited suggestions and important advice.'

Lockhart also discerned the quality of Miss Rigby's letters of
travel:

'I have been reading the manuscript with great admiration
for the most part,' he told Murray. 'I wish the lady would score
out a few fine words, but beyond these trifles she is unassailable.
I have no doubt she is the cleverest female now in England, the
most original in thought and expression too; she seems *good*
besides, which after all has its charms even for old sinners like you
and me. She is really quite first-rate in her pictures, and in her
little disquisitions too.'

This was passed on to the author, now at home again in Framlingham; she found it deeply gratifying, 'altho' my poor judgement cannot be induced to concur with that of Mr. Lockhart in
the matter of approbation. But what excites the good opinion of
such a critic has made me very happy by proving that the kindness and liberality with which you accepted a work of which you
had seen so small a portion, may not have been misplaced. For I
can say with entire truth that the only part of my work which
affords me any pride is the circumstance of its being published by
Mr. Murray'.

The lady may be thought to protest too much. She did not at
any time undervalue her own work.

'It is rather strange to think that Mr. Lockhart's Life of Sir
W. Scott is the only work of importance I perused during the
progress of my writing, and I was often made aware of its useful
influence. Certain it is that I concluded the work with a profound veneration for Sir Walter, and a lively desire to become
acquainted with his biographer.'

She approved the title: *A Residence on the Shores of the Baltic
Described in a Series of Letters* but not the addition, 'By a Lady',
and recurred to this point more than ten years later when a new
edition was being prepared: 'I think that the ladylike origin is not

felt generally to be any recommendation to a volume.' Her book
was reviewed in *The Quarterly Review* in September 1841:

'Here we have the results of close feminine observance in
a new sphere, set down with such an easy, unaffected grace of
language as might have given great attraction to a delineation
of the most hackneyed scenery and the most familiar manners.'
The review gave copious quotations; and praised the courage of
the author during that storm at sea: 'It is a picture that calls up
the true glow of patriotic pride.' The reviewer found that 'so
many indications of the writer's own character are uncon-
sciously given that the reader's admiration and respect are at once
excited and enchained at the outset'. He commended also her
adaptability and sympathy:

'This lady, so far from adopting the contemptuous tone
usual with French and English tourists in Russia, appears to give
the government of the Emperor Nicholas credit for a most
sincere zeal in promoting the welfare and happiness of the people.'

Finally, after quoting her description of the Russian spring,
he concluded benignly:

'Here we stop, though with reluctance—but we feel that we
have already drawn on this rich bank quite as deeply as we could
in fairness do. The writer's name will not long, we suppose, remain a secret—and we trust no engagements in Esthonia or else-
where may prevent us from seeing it—or a *quid pro quo*—on many
a title-page hereafter.'

The justly gratified author wrote to her publisher:

'A notice therein is in itself an honour, and further, the manner
in which I was treated is so undeservedly flattering that I cannot
but think your press exercises an improving influence no less over
the matter than the form of a MS. Such being the case you may
be sure that I shall not be unwilling to trouble you again.' She
made only one slight criticism:

'I would rather he had left my "elder sister, the expatriated
Baroness" alone whom he has introduced to the public more distinctly than I have done.' The reviewer had mentioned the

domestic circumstances of the visit. 'However, it was perhaps needful to assign some respectable motive to my wanderings which otherwise hardly assimilate with the appended name of "spinster"!'

Lockhart invited her to write for *The Quarterly*.

'Were I to attend only to my own suggestions, these would tell me I might aspire to illustrating his *Ballads*, but certainly not to appearing in his *Quarterly*.' Lockhart had made a name for himself by his spirited translation of *Spanish Ballads* published by Murray. An obvious subject for Miss Rigby soon occurred: she was asked to review three volumes of travel in Russia—by Khöl, Jesse, and Sterling respectively—in *The Quarterly* of April 1842.

'Signora Estonia has most cleverly extended her paper, and made it quite what will do her and the Q.R. credit'—so Lockhart told Murray. To the author herself he wrote:

'You are the only lady, I believe, that ever wrote in it except Mrs. Somerville who once gave us a short, scientific article. I had long felt and regretted the want of that knowledge of women and their concerns, which men can never attain, for the handling of numberless questions most interesting and most important to society.'

It was the beginning of a true friendship. Lockhart and she had artistic as well as literary gifts in common. 'The pencil is the child of my heart,' she once declared, and Lockhart who himself drew deftly and wittily, praised her drawings; but urged the claims of 'pen against pencil; £1,000 to an orange', and her career justified his advice. His encouragement and Murray's fanned the small flame of her talent into a steady glow:

'I can only wish that all novices like myself might fall into such kind and encouraging hands,' she told John Murray; and when favourable notices of her book began to appear, admitted with candour:

'I find myself swallowing all the good things the reviewers say of me with considerable relish, and imputing their criticisms to any misconception of style and judgement save to my own;

for which arrogance I deserve the severest of animadversions in my eyes, namely a reproof from yourself.'

Her relations with both publisher and editor were from the first friendly, and mutually sympathetic. She was one of the few who saw beyond Lockhart's reserve and satiric humour the goodness and integrity that won and held his friends: the qualities Scott had discerned in him:

'With the most chilling reserve he has the most genuine openness; and with the stiffest bearing the purest simplicity. . . . No man estimates real goodness so highly, or holds false goodness so cheaply. His pride and stiffness are independent of rank, station, intellect and person. He is prouder of the name of Lockhart than of all the distinction he has given it. This is a regular Scotch feeling.'

She wrote thus from Edinburgh, where she proved the truth of this last assertion by seeing it in reverse. At a dinner party she sat beside Sir Norman Lockhart, M.P. for Lanarkshire, and having asked if he were of the same family as Scott's biographer was informed stiffly: 'He is of my family.'

She looked on Lockhart with an artist's eye:

'It is a pleasure to see him think. . . . There never was a face with so little of the animal in it; the features, too, spiritualized—one hardly knows whether most sharpened by care or refined by intellect.' She noted 'the great contrasts of expression; excessive sourness and ineffable sweetness, the small, lipless mouth giving the one, the beautiful, soft-lashed eyes the other'.

Life was expanding for Miss Rigby. Framlingham was near Norwich where she found agreeable society, especially at the Palace with the Bishop and his family—his son Arthur, later Dean Stanley, and his daughter Catherine. She was still drawing upon her memories and impressions of Estonia, and wrote a story, 'The Wolves', for *Fraser's Magazine*; Murray published another story, *The Jewess*, and a volume of *Livonian Tales*. Success was sweet and she was grateful:

'I think all your authors ought to club together, and spare a

portion off each of their lives to prolong the life of one infinitely
more valuable' she wrote to the Emperor on his birthday. In the
Christmas of 1841, the year of the publication of the *Letters*,
she sent him a long, formal document, purporting to be a translation and report of a resolution passed by the Ritterschaft of
Lithuania at 'the last Landstag, of passing you a public vote of
thanks' for having published the said volume.

> 'It is true that owing
> First to an ignorance of the English language,
> Second to a national objection to much reading,
> Third to not having read the work at all,

they are by no means certain what it is all about. Nevertheless,
from the high repute in which your name stands and which has
penetrated far beyond the shores of the Baltic, they feel assured
that you would publish nothing which did not greatly redound to
your credit and their own; and, it would seem, entertain a far
greater confidence in the publisher than in the writer of the book
in question.'

Apparently, various ways of honouring Mr. Murray had been
discussed:

(1) His adoption into the matriculated nobility of Lithuania:
this was rejected as involving proof of thirty-two quarterings,
which it would be an insult to demand of an Englishman.

(2) Making him a member of the Schwarzen Häupter: rejected because of the inconvenience of the armoured uniform.

(3) Sending him a gift of money: rejected, because to send
money to wealthy England was like sending coals to Newcastle
or owls to Athens!

Finally it was resolved to present him with a gift for the palate;
and so that rare bird *Gallina Icenorum* was being dispatched. In
short, as Mr. Micawber would put it, Miss Rigby was sending
him a Norfolk turkey.

Murray presented her with a set of Byron's Works and a copy
of Thomas Moore's *Life of Byron*.

'When I was young,' she wrote in acknowledgement, 'Byron was my *beau idéal* of men and poets; but then cares came over me, and my *beau idéal* only made bad worse. . . . Moore's *Life* put the finishing blow to my enthusiasm. Now, however, that I have seen more of life, have been in the company of the Emperor of Russia, Mr. Murray, and the Bishop of Norwich, and thus strengthened my mind without extinguishing my fancy, I return to him with a double zest, and enjoy him the more because I pity him the less. . . . I think it gives some definition of the respective characters of Byron and Scott to say that each could equally have engrossed a woman's heart; but the former it would have been the greatest misfortune in the world to have loved, the latter the greatest privilege.'

IV

EDINBURGH AND THE SCOTS

IN the 1840's Elizabeth began keeping a journal, at first chiefly of reflections, then more and more of events and experiences. There is a hint of her inner life, of private grief, of faith and self-discipline:

'Certain feelings follow from certain positions. They must have exercise somewhere, and if they are denied entrance in the right mind then they force it in the wrong.' There may have been a disappointment in love, a loss and grief, a frustration.

'Why do men invariably judge better than women? Simply because their feelings have less interference'—or less inhibition as we should say.

'Everything that tends to diminish the sense of protection given and received between man and woman is bad. Woman is made to lean, man to support'—and her own very feminine household may have appeared to lack this balance. Her own strong and resourceful character had still an instinctive desire for protection. This part of her journal reveals her as introspective. Her published work and her later journal both show her as, in modern terms an extrovert; but this came by discipline as well as by nature:

'Self-forgetfulness and self-possession are the extremes which meet; they are essential to all excellence,' and the first of them could be won by activity.

'The heavy heart is best carried on the fleet foot. It is best to see your sorrows as large as life, and acquaint yourself with them face to face; often they lose as much by this process as the mind gains. Those who feel and grapple with their griefs deserve our sympathy; those who cheat themselves our pity.'

She had escaped Wertherism; her youthful visit to Germany

at what might have been too impressionable an age had merely disciplined her mind; she had been mentally vaccinated against self-pity.

'There is no simplicity so simple as that which is refined; no sorrow so touching as that which is subdued; no art so beautiful as that which is concealed.' She was a child more of the classic than the romantic period; art and morals were inextricably interwoven in her mind:

'There is more moral courage in refusing than in accepting, and more merit in restricting genius than in indulging it.'

In the midst of the evangelical movement she held to a sober way of faith: 'Defend me from your very humble people; like persons who go about turning their toes in and poking their backs out and not venturing to lift their feet from the ground, they are sure to entangle themselves and tumble down in their own awkward low-mindedness; the consequence is that others are at the trouble of picking them up, and propping them ever after.'

Like a sound woman of the world she believed in keeping conscience in its place and ignoring scruples:

'There have been as many errors committed in the name of conscience as there have been crimes in the name of liberty. . . . It seems to be forgotten that this quality, like every other in the human breast, is fallible, and as such open to as much sinful perversion as it is capable of sound cultivation. . . . We should do with conscience as with a woman's affections—so train the mind that she misplace not the treasure.'

At a time when the godly tended to be gloomy and to bemoan the fallen state of man, she insisted on Christian cheerfulness: 'True religion, to do good, should sit easily upon the heart. . . . The best proof of the mind's being in a state of grace, and the best argument in favour of that religion is the happiness it obviously affords.'

Whatever pain there may have been in her inner life was mastered, whatever crisis, passed, when in 1842 the Rigby ladies went to Edinburgh, there to make their home for seven years.

They took a house or possibly lodgings in St. Bernard's Crescent, whence Elizabeth wrote cheerfully to John Murray of their enjoyment of Edinburgh society. Thanks to introductions from him (he kept his Scots connections and he had married a Scots wife, Anne Elliot) and from Lockhart—'we are gradually making our way into that improving and rational kind [of society] we most desire'—though not so improving as to be dull. Nothing can be less accurate than to picture early Victorian Edinburgh as sunk in godly gloom or fettered by prim gentility. The glow of the golden age still lingered; there were wits and characters. Edinburgh parties were a revelation to this English-woman, with their tradition of good talk and uninhibited merri-ment well maintained. At one dinner Elizabeth sat beside the Dean of the Faculty of Law 'who so much amused me that I could hardly laugh within the bounds of decorum. It was too much to look at him and hear him both'. Everywhere she found 'perfect ease, much spirited conversation, ample board and hearty welcomes'.

She met men who had known Scott: Lord Jeffrey, Professor Wilson (Christopher North of the *Noctes Ambrosianae* and of *Blackwood's Magazine* in the riotous early days of *Maga* when he, Lockhart and James Hogg wrote their pungent reviews and scandalous articles). She found Wilson a great, leonine personage with his mane of white hair 'looking like a wild man, and talking like the most polished, excellent man'. Jeffrey, little and spruce, a tiny terror of a critic, came to call 'looking as sharp as a needle and as fresh as a rose'. They had long been political opponents; Wilson a deep-dyed Tory, Jeffrey as bellicose a Whig as ever enlivened *The Edinburgh Review*. These passions were somewhat spent now, but the two friendly rivals in letters were still con-trasted: 'The little lord was small and delicate and dainty in build,' Elizabeth recalled long afterwards, and prided himself on speaking English. Wilson had 'a tremendous burr' and Scots accent. Jeffrey was immaculate in appearance, almost dainty; Wilson 'a notorious slut'.

The Edinburgh gentry, literary, legal and county, were most hospitable; chief among them were Sir John and Lady MacNeill, she being a sister of Professor Wilson, the Swintons of the old Berwickshire family, the Gartshores. Mrs. Gartshore was a sweet singer and a charming hostess.

The Rigbys made many friends and soon felt at home. 'But mamma and her butcher can't come to right terms at all'—no doubt because he kept offering her hough and gigots and other mysterious cuts. 'Our manservant also who by no means does discredit to the Norfolk accent is very indignant because the Scotch housemaid says he can't speak English.'

Edinburgh talk was then, as always, full of racy memories. There were many living links with the past besides Wilson and Jeffrey: 'Mr. Murray of Henderland had been in Sir Joshua's study, and Jeffrey had helped to carry Boswell drunk to bed.' Miss Rigby heard reminiscences of Scott, of Henry Mackenzie whose novel *The Man of Feeling*, so influential in its day, is now so unreadable, but whose own memoirs of his boyhood and youth are so delightful; of Sydney Smith once a light of *The Edinburgh Review*, now Canon of St. Paul's. She met an old lady, Miss Goldie, whose mother had given Scott the story of Jeanie Deans for *The Heart of Midlothian*—'The one novel most fitted to please and edify a woman'.

Lockhart was well remembered in this society; it was only sixteen years since he had left it for London, and these men were his friends. Miss Rigby found that he was 'liked, nay loved, by his intimates; but a rooted shyness stood between him and mere acquaintances with whom he was never popular. He had a way, too, of calling things by their right names which did not suit at all'. His manner, in public, lacked cordiality: a finger instead of a hand held out in greeting, 'the stiffest of all possible backs' and the slightest of smiles on 'the small, sarcastic mouth'. But he was a true friend to his own: 'No man might be slower to profess friendship, but none surer to keep it.'

Edinburgh society had moved from the steep 'lands' of the

Old Town to the elegant houses of the New, set in classically designed Squares, Places and Circuses: houses 'some of the most commodious that ever were built . . . favourable to a society which was not hurried and never a crush'.

Political feeling no longer rose to fever pitch, 'and the rancours of the Free Kirk which were in full force did not appear in general society'. The Disruption—in which a large body of ministers and laity broke away from the Established Kirk in protest against any form of State rule, shown, particularly in patronage—found more adherents in the Whiggish West of Scotland; more among the wealthy merchants of Glasgow than among the legal, professional and landed gentry of Edinburgh, some of whom, indeed, were downright, unashamed Episcopalians.

The Rigbys appear to have returned to Norfolk for a time in the summer; but 'I am returning to the land of inspiration' Elizabeth told John Murray, and having returned in the early autumn wrote to him:

'Edinburgh is filling now, and Princes Street looks less like Piccadilly deserted. George Street, Great King Street and others are still almost entirely abandoned to bands of schoolboys who play lengthways and crossways without the slightest fear of interruption. Altogether Edinburgh is a wonderful mart for children if you know of anyone wanting a few.'

The dinner and supper parties were resumed. At one she met the immense and exuberant Lord of Session, Lord Robertson, a friend of Lockhart, a wit and raconteur:

'He made me laugh till I was almost shocked to hear myself, with stories of all the wits and poets of the time. He is quite one of the lions of the capital. . . . I understand he was also amused with me, but I do not understand when he found time for that.'

Professor Wilson also 'announces to the world that he is very much in love with me, and that if, by accident, I should be reminded of his age by hearing his grandchildren cry, he shall tell me "it is only the cat"'. She liked the swashbuckler in him. He

D

said once that 'if he was sure to have a verdict of insane brought, there were nine men in Edinburgh whom he should be delighted to shoot'. Another quotation from him was his definition of a man whom everyone likes: 'A damned blockhead but a perfect gentleman.'

He proved, on more intimate knowledge, to be 'good and religious as well as witty and poetic' and she thought he 'would be venerable if his hair were within bounds'.

Miss Rigby enjoyed her respectable flirtations which were extended, by letter, to her publisher:

'I am perfectly aware that Lady Sale has taken that position in your affections which, with her military knowledge, she will not fail securely to establish. I shall have to get in again by stratagem if at all.'

Lady Sale was the wife of the great Indian officer, General Sir Robert Sale, defender of Jalalabad. She had been with him through siege and campaign, in every peril and hardship, a most valiant soldier's wife. Her *Journal of the Disasters in Afghanistan* was published by Murray in 1843.

Miss Rigby was an adroit picker-up of *obiter dicta*, mostly those of witty intellectuals; but one saying which deeply moved her was heard at no party; it was spoken by an old woman who had lost three sons:

'My Willie's death opened such a gap in my heart that his brothers seemed to slip through unfelt.'

Life in Edinburgh was genial, even gay. Balls and assemblies were lively, and the reels danced there impressed, even startled this Englishwoman:

'Young men and children, old men and maidens all jumping, whirling and toiling alike. You can hardly believe your eyes till you see the oldest and gravest in the land cutting capers, snapping fingers, tossing their heads, twisting round, brandishing their arms, shaking their legs, clapping hands, whooping, yelling and screaming till you expect them to sink down with sheer exhaustion like dervishes. The older they get, the more mad do the gentlemen become.'

The MacNeills gave a masked ball which Elizabeth and a group of friends chose to attend dressed as little girls in pink cotton frocks with white 'tidies' or pinafores. Their arrival caused a sensation among the spectators at the door: 'See the bonny wee bairns!'

The bairns were all well-grown young women, and one of them at least, Elizabeth herself, was more than common tall. Lockhart's nickname for her was 'Lofty Lucy'. For Edinburgh of the Free Kirk, of long sermons and intolerable Sabbaths this was, as the man in the gallery said of Mrs. Siddons as Lady Macbeth—'No' bad'.

But there was plenty of church-going besides. Episcopacy was by now fairly prevalent, having emerged from the shadows of persecution and suppression, and it was tending to mellow the atmosphere of the city in which it was tolerated. That the godly could be genial was proved by the Bishop, Dr. Terrot—'French by name, origin and vivacity', English by birth, amiable in character. It was said of him that had he been completely French he might have been another Fenélon. 'No,' said the Bishop with candour, 'I should have been a scoundrel.' He was once asked for his disapproval of a charity ball, but disconcerted the seekers of censure by his reply:

'I am sure if it could do anyone any good, I'd dance down the whole length of George Street in full canonicals.'

Dean Ramsay was no less genial. He was Rector of St. John the Evangelist's Church which the Rigbys attended. (Deans in the Scots Episcopal Church have a diocesan office and authority; the head of the Cathedral Chapter is the Provost.) The Dean was 'tenderly persuasive in the pulpit and a fascinating converser' according to Miss Rigby, and his memory is still vivid. He left a delightful volume of *Recollections of Scottish Life* and his stories still circulate.

Something of the old prejudice against the theatre lingered. Mrs. Walford, that popular Victorian novelist who spent her girlhood in Edinburgh, recalled that her family, ruled by the discipline of the Free Kirk, did not got to the theatre. Concerts were approved, and there were balls and parties enough to make girlhood gay. Miss Rigby found that people would go to see a star like Rachel, but that few of them had the habit of theatre-going.

Concerts were popular as they had been half a century and more before, in the great days of St. Cecilia's Hall. Miss Rigby found them second-rate, and preferred the musical parties given by ladies like Mrs. Gartshore; the season she spent in Edinburgh, coming in from her country house was called the Gartshore Festival. These parties were not too large, and one could enjoy good music in comfort, uncrowded. One singer failed to please. She had 'an immense voice, warranted 300 yards, like a reel of thread but just as thin and wiry'.

Sermon-tasting was still part of social life, as well as the discussion of books and music. The Scot went to church as the Frenchmen to the play, the Italian to the opera, the Spaniard to the bull-fight, the Englishman to any game or sport; he went to hear, sometimes to admire, always to criticize. Miss Rigby followed this example and criticized freely. Her own clergy did not escape: 'wordy, fuzzy sermons' she noted of the preaching of the curate at St. John's. She was free from so-called ecumenical tendencies but her journalistic curiosity led her occasionally to Presbyterian kirks, always in a spirit unmuffled by Christian charity.

Having gone to hear Dr. Guthrie in his 'conventicle' she found 'the place full of most decent-looking people, but all the Scotch look decent on a Sunday'; but she was shocked by the preacher's 'cringing to the people and telling them they were able to judge, for it was the people with whom Christ was popular, and the elders and higher classes who persecuted. I wonder who it was that crucified Him. He attacked the Bishops and the Apostolic Succession with all the vulgarity and narrowness of mind with which an Evangelical clergyman will attack the Papists . . . a perfect agitator and an excellent specimen of how the pulpit is made use of to quicken the worst species of pride in the Scottish mob'.

In June 1843 she spent a holiday in Dunoon on the Firth of Clyde, already a popular resort, and from thence went on a tour of the Highlands. The packet-boat on the Clyde was full of an odd mixture of people: 'Scotch children are extraordinary—heads and legs bare, and the rest as well-dressed as a child of higher station; women with smart flowers in their hats and striped petti-coats under their flannel gowns.' Equally odd was the German lady, on another excursion, who was dressed dowdily in satin: 'The Germans never wear a decently made common dress.'

In Dunoon she attended the Free Kirk in a 'non-Intrusionist box' which reminded her of 'a theatre-booth at a fair—the same kind of rough seats and sawdust, a wooden box at one end and a painted dressing-table before it'—not the most seemly way of referring to the Communion-table. The men had 'old, sturdy, hard-burnt, rocky faces . . . which seemed never to have had reverence for man or sentiment for women—contumacious and obstinate all over'.

As an artist she was fascinated by physical aspects, and else-where in her Journal noted two types of Scottish face: one large, raw and bony, reddish in colouring; the other, the Celtic type, small, clear of complexion, with black hair: 'a face of no softness and no openness, but intensely shrewd and intellectual, and one which you are long in trusting and never tired of examining'. The women on one occasion were seen to have 'wide-open faces, with their features, the moment they speak, flopping back like the borders of their caps'.

On a minor excursion in Edinburgh itself, out to Roslin to see the chapel, she found that exotic flower of the late Renaissance a 'luscious conglomeration, that inlaid cabinet of all the imaginable sweets of architecture, that *potpourri*, that *biscuitwork* of composi-tion . . . a very fancy ball of architecture.'

In vigour of language she was fully qualified to be a contributor to *The Quarterly Review*, whose pages did not lack pungency.

This year, 1843, saw the death of her old friend and publisher, John Murray the Second.

'No one can succeed him in some respects, but in all that concerns the stability of the great publishing house, his son is quite fitted to take his place. He is an admirable young man, and though not what his father was, he will be that which he was not.'

The friendship was to continue. John the Third was of her own age, thirty-four. He lived with his mother in the house in Albemarle Street, and there Miss Rigby was soon to be their guest. Meanwhile she spent another autumn and winter in Edinburgh, very delightfully and very busily.

V

WRITING FOR *THE QUARTERLY*

THESE years in Edinburgh were indeed active professionally, when Miss Rigby built solidly upon the foundation of fame laid by her *Letters From the Baltic*. She was writing her long and scholarly articles for *The Quarterly Review*, in a *genre* now well-established among men of letters, but scarcely attempted by women.

The first of these was the review, already mentioned, in March 1842, of three books on Russia: *Notes of a Half-Pay Officer in Search of Health; or, Russia, Circassia and the Crimea in* 1839–40, by Captain Jesse; *Russia Under Nicholas the First,* translated by Anthony Sterling; and a volume of drawings by the German artist von Köhl. This was less of a review than a travel article, deriving as much from the writer's own memories as from the books under survey. It was full and well informed, and for the most part she approved of the books. From her own experience she could agree with Captain Jesse's strictures on Russian officials: all dishonest and all on the make. She could not, however, accept his description of the peasants as dull, stupid and super-stitious; on the contrary, she had found them loyal and pious, shrewd, witty and gay, with a love of colour and of song: 'at once active and tractable, intelligent and confiding, their affection more developed than their knowledge'—too little know, and well worth knowing. She disagreed, also, with the dismissal of the Russian Church as merely superstitious. It had, indeed, many corruptions, but 'who will not prefer a soil choked with rubbish to one too sterile for even the weeds of faith to find nourishment?' She was thinking of the Lutheranism she had found in the Baltic Province, and heartily disliked.

Her article on *German Ladies*, quoted earlier, links the young, observant Elizabeth with the mature journalist. These journeys in Germany and Russia had given her a lien over German and Russian subjects; but she had discovered another territory—that of books for children. These were beginning to appear in profusion. 'Looked over children's books', she noted one day. Many come within my ban—artful instruction and artificial amusement; the one not avowed and the other not genuine.'

She wrote three articles for *The Quarterly* on these books: in December 1842, in May 1843, and June 1844 respectively. The same thread runs through them all: a deprecation of intrusive morality and didacticism, of affected playfulness, of talking down. She found in many of the new, improving little books for the young a bad mixture of instruction and amusement:

'We do not know when they are at work or at play', and the normal child instinctively knew that difference, realized the need for application to plain learning, and would not 'really thank you for dressing up his studies in a trifling or jocose manner'. Most children liked books 'beyond their years', and would rather work hard in the schoolroom, then be released for play unshadowed by learning, than have lessons served as entertainment.

'Children . . . are gifted with an exquisite tact for detecting dull passages, and are as sure to avoid the hook as to relish the bait.' They would rightly dislike those horrid little books where 'subjects of the highest difficulty are chattered over between two disgusting little prodigies, or delivered to them in mouthfuls . . . by a learned mother'. She was denouncing American books in general and one in particular: Gollaudet's *Child's Book of the Soul*, in which a mother and child discussed theology, mamma thus expounding Divine Holiness:

'God never did one wrong or wicked thing. . . . He never did so, ever so little. He never thought, ever so little, to do so. God is displeased ever so little of doing so.'

Miss Rigby commented: 'If Americans will know all about

God's thoughts, with reverence be it said that it might be as well to put them in decent syntax, and do more credit to their country-man, Lindley Murray'—the grammarian. These American juvenilia were denounced as 'transatlantic abominations'; a series of Peter Parley volumes as absurd, the *Rollo* stories as dull and pedantic, uncouth in style with 'crack-jaw words and puritan-derived expressions'.

A child's imagination as well as his brain must be fed: 'Healthy enjoyment brings profit and develops the mind'—and tales of heroism and fidelity did more than preaching to edify as well as delight the young reader.

In her second article she returned to the charge with fresh vigour and a well-sharpened spear. She was reviewing Mrs. Sherwood's *Lady of the Manor, Being a Series of Conversations on the Subject of Confirmation Intended for the Use of the Middle and Upper Ranks of Young Females.* As this impressive work was published in seven volumes, the lower ranks were not likely to be interested. It was a new and enlarged edition of what had originally appeared in parts, between 1825 and 1829.

The Lady of the Manor was an elderly gentlewoman endowed with every spiritual grace and with worldly wealth besides, which makes a most comfortable provision for this life and the next. The vicar of the parish was 'a young man of humble and teachable disposition' (otherwise he would not have been given the living), so diffident about his own power to instruct and his own spiritual authority that he had begged the Lady to prepare the young gentlewomen of the neighbourhood for confirmation, while he, apparently, tackled the village wenches.

The Lady's teaching was enforced and illustrated by tales of worldly folly and vice intended to be a warning, but much more likely to prove an enticement. The Lady, in fact, put ideas into the heads of her hearers, and Miss Rigby pronounced that sooner would she see girls reading the silliest novels than those solemn and pious volumes that had 'so much of positive evil'.

She is at her most pungent and best in this article. For most amateurs of early Victoriana and of pious literature, Mrs. Sherwood is now only the author of *The Fairchild Family*, which can still be enjoyed in parts, though by no means in the spirit intended by the author. *The Lady of the Manor* would probably defeat the most ardent lover of period flavour; but in Miss Rigby's potted versions the tales can entertain and startle us. There was plenty of vice, particularly among the aristocracy, and we might possibly find here the first bad baronet or wicked marquis, the heartless beauty and the peeress whose morals were as spotted as her ermine. In fact, Mrs. Sherwood emerges as an author of first-class melodrama, if only her piety could be swallowed with her plots. Heroines rode to hounds with hat plumes waving in the breeze, danced at a ball, caught a chill and died; the white plumes of the hearse were then seen waving even where the hat-plumes had fluttered a week before. Others went driving to the races, were thrown out of the phaeton and crippled for life; others tried to poison an innocent but wealthy cousin.

Many of the stories were in the first person, told as confessions, with a 'morbid pleasure in the most extravagant self-condemnation', and these Miss Rigby crisply described as 'pious auto-anatomists'.

The detective novel, as we know it, had not yet occurred; otherwise Miss Rigby might have found in Mrs. Sherwood a treasure-trove of plots.

The religious element was the most nauseating of all, being administered like a medicine smothered in the jam of a story or pseudo-play: 'We have no faith in young ladies who talk of "flowers and seeds and happy deaths in the parish", and we have no patience with little boys who quote long passages from the Psalms of David then "topple heels over head", or who talk of "that pretty chapter in the Hebrews" and then make ducks and drakes.'

The most famous of Miss Rigby's future victims, Charlotte Brontë, would have agreed with her in this. It is strange that in her bitter review, some years later, of *Jane Eyre*, she failed to note and enjoy the small Jane's account of Mr. Brocklehurst's little son. When offered his choice between a psalm to learn and a ginger-nut to eat, that astute child chose the psalm, because: 'Angels sing psalms, and I wish to be a little angel here below'; and was then given two ginger-nuts as reward for his infant piety.

Miss Rigby had no patience with intrusive piety, infant, adolescent, or adult. With her robust liking for the world, her sympathy with youthful gaiety, she found that good fiction could edify as well as entertain the reader by making virtue attractive. Scott and other novelists 'by infusing a healthy tone into the whole frame of public taste, may be said to guard those valuable outworks through which all enemies to religion must first pass'.

The gay might be good; happiness was not sinful or even silly, and often the 'apparent inanities of visiting' and other pastimes imposed by convention had value as discipline. They might be 'as conducive to the ends of charity and self-denial as greater exertions or greater trials'. Certainly the Victorian girl had every opportunity for such discipline. The way of courtesy could be hard.

The Evangelical contempt for the world was 'so much the more dangerous as being levelled against an immense community of baptized and communicating Christians who, because surrounded with all the apparel of hereditary wealth or nobility, are sweepingly condemned by those who move at too great distance from them in society to know how they bestow the one or adorn the other'. There was a 'religious dissipation' as well as the worldly kind, and it was quite as bad and dangerous 'as regards the length of time devoted, the necessary absences from home duties, the heart-burnings, envyings and jealousies, and the vanity of seeing and being seen' as were any of the gaieties, 'balls or plays which were attended with such fatal consequences for Mrs. Sherwood's heroines.'

The Lady of the Manor contained *romans jeune fille* (of a sort) rather than stories for children. The latter were appearing in abundance, and in June 1844 Miss Rigby reviewed a varied batch. One must wish that she had tried her own hand in this *genre*. She had a lively style, considerable narrative power, and extremely sound ideas:

'The most obvious rule in writing for the amusement or instruction of childhood is to bear in mind that it is not the extremes of genius or dullness which we are to address' but the ordinary; 'that large class of average ability to be found in children of healthy mental and physical formation'.

Again she denounced that 'idolatry of teaching' in season and out of season which was so prevalent, and the 'wishy-washy materials' of which many juvenile books were made. A child had better read something beyond than beneath his immediate understanding. Indiscriminate reading was healthy; children had 'an instinct of food which more cultivated palates lose', and could pick up scraps of knowledge and delight as they browsed. Most children disliked 'cut down books', extracts and simplifications; 'Glimpses of this, Gleanings of that, Footsteps to the other.' They rightly preferred to do their own editing, to skip as they pleased, and they appeared to 'possess an inherent conviction that when the hole is big enough for the cat, no smaller one at the side is needed for the kitten'.

Children's books were not the same thing as childish books. There was a world of difference, and there could be an interchange of reading, happy and profitable for both, between grown-ups and children: the one side reading or re-reading the good old fairy tales and romances; the other discovering the grown-up classics in poetry and fiction, thus laying up treasure for their life's enjoyment.

Her mind must have gone back to her own happy and untrammelled childhood in Norwich and Framlingham, to the open bookcase with well-filled shelves, the old, beloved tales, the good, new novels, the poetry and drama, and books of travel.

A few books were denounced: *Conversations with Mamma* by Mrs. Marshall who was of the school of Mrs. Sherwood; various volumes of Glimpses and Gleanings; *The Children's Friend; The Juvenile Manual; Aids to Development.*

The recommendations far outnumbered the condemnations. Among them was what must have been an enchanting anthology (fore-runner of Walter de la Mare's): *The House Treasury* compiled by Felix Summerley, containing Nursery Songs and Tales. *Aesop's Fables* were essential to any good nursery or schoolroom library; and there were Gay's *Fables*, and a collection by G. G. Keene of *Persian Fables.* In poetry there were Jane and Ann Taylor, Isaac Watts, Mrs. Hemans, and *The Christian Year*, then very new but already part of a child's Sunday reading.

There must, of course, be books of instruction: pure instruction, not the kind that were mixed with a sickly jam of forced entertainment. Miss Edgeworth's many volumes were admirable; *Evenings at Home* (by Mrs. Barbauld and Dr. Aiken) was commended, and Mrs. Trimmer's *History of the Robins*—already a classic—was warmly praised.

A group of nature books included White's *History of Selborne*, Goldsmith's *Animated Nature*, and various books about birds, country life, fishing, with some stories about *Dogs, Horses, Travellers and Shipwrecks*: a most alluring omnibus.

Washington Irving's *Columbus* and Southey's *Nelson* were excellent biographies, and for schoolroom or lesson-books there were Mrs. Markham, Miss Mangnall (with her *Questions*), Goldsmith for history, Lindley Murray for grammer, Scott's enchanting *Tales of a Grandfather*, and the book that had suggested them—*Stories From English History* by the fearsome Croker himself.

Solid instruction was necessary, but there must always be a flow of stories, of this world or of faery: Grimm—with Cruickshank's illustrations—a collection of Irish legends by the other, more agreeable Croker—Thomas Crofton; Lamb's *Tales From Shakespeare* and his *Ulysses.*

Miss Rigby had apparently a healthy taste for tales of adventure and recommended *Feats on the Fiord* and *The Crofton Boys* by that formidable fellow-journalist and fellow-countrywoman Harriet Martineau. *Robinson Crusoe* must be in every bookcase, with *Masterman Ready* that 'best of *Robinson Crusoe's* numerous descendants'—so delightful that parents were likely to filch it from their children.

For romance and fantasy there were *Phantasmion* by Mrs. Henry Coleridge, and de la Motte Fouqué's *Undine*, which was so beloved by generations of Victorian youth in real life and in fiction.

Scotland had produced two much-loved authors in Catherine Sinclair with her *Holiday House*, and Ann Fraser Tytler with *Leila on the Island* and its sequels.

For religious reading there were, in addition to the hymns and devout poems, *The Pilgrim's Progress*—'the sooner read the better', with a number of now forgotten or half-forgotten tales by Wilberforce, Hannah More and others, including Charlotte Yonge's friend and inspirer Marianne Dyson, whose *Ivo and Verona* was much praised.

It is a substantial bill of fare, and it includes delights as well as nourishment. A child could and should read both for learning and for fun. But there must be no false whimsy, no writing down, no cheating on the part of the author. Mind, heart and imagination were alike fed. The child was set free in a large room.

Miss Rigby was, if one may so put it, a numerous aunt, and probably a delightful one. Her opinions and selection may have been influenced by recent knowledge of her nephews and nieces as well by memory and personal taste. Indulging briefly and apologetically in whimsy, we can see her dispatching large parcels of books, review copies among them, to the nursery in Reval.

VI

VARIED SCENES. LONDON: TRAVEL: EDINBURGH

THE pleasant life in Edinburgh had a happy interruption early in 1844, when Elizabeth went to London to stay for three months with John Murray the Third and his mother. No. 50 Albemarle Street was becoming more and more the resort of men and women of letters. At Mrs. Murray's dinner-table Elizabeth met old friends and made some new, among them the Carlyles. She liked them both; Mrs. Carlyle was 'the more refined half' but he was 'an honest, true man, a character such as he himself alone can describe. He is a kind of Burns in appearance—the head of a thinker, the eye of a lover, the mouth of a peasant'. The second attribute has usually been overlooked in Carlyle and may explain some of the complications of his married life. Elizabeth and he got on very happily until he pronounced Luther 'a nice man' to which she retorted 'there was nothing nice about him'. Some days later she visited Cheyne Row, and her liking for her hosts there increased:

'I never felt myself in more intellectual society—such knowledge and such equal originality. Mrs. Carlyle interested me. She is lively and clever and evidently very happy' which is comfortable hearing about 'that ever diverse pair' who were so strongly bound together. Carlyle, his guest found 'had the thinnest possible surface to his mind; you can get through it at once' and that was the secret of his misery and self-tormenting, as of his genius. You could get through at once to the nerves of pain. But it was no morose philosopher that Elizabeth met: 'the best laugh I ever heard, and I doubt not a tear in season'.

Lockhart and his daughter Charlotte dined at No. 50; Lockhart widowed some years earlier, and finding increasing comfort and companionship in this girl who, at sixteen, had a maturity of mind and character beyond her years. An old grand-aunt wrote of her that she was 'a delightful girl, an extraordinary likeness of both mother and poor Anne, but with the extreme gentleness of Sophia. There has been great care bestowed on her education, and with much success, indeed Mr. Lockhart has been one of the best of fathers'.

With her mother's gentleness and feminine intelligence, Charlotte had a good deal of her father's intellect, and was in every way a worthy grandchild to Sir Walter Scott. Since her mother's death she had been under the care of a governess Miss Watkins, who seems to have been far superior to the run of that often despised and sometimes incompetent class. Charlotte was fluent in French, Italian and German, and was solidly well read, with much stimulus from her father. Lockhart's letters to her when she was in Brighton or in Scotland with her governess or at a *pensionnat* in France, are among the most endearing documents of his life. He wrote to her affectionately, amusingly, never condescendingly, with news and gossip as if to a mature woman, not as to a fledgeling.

About this time the long, affectionate relationship with Miss Watkins was broken, and Miss Rigby, in all innocence, may have had something to do with it. Lockhart wrote to his son Walter that Miss Watkins was being difficult, 'tift' or piqued by imagined slights. Miss Rigby had dined with them, and as a distinguished guest and contributor to his *Quarterly* had, naturally, been treated with particular attention and deference: with more than was shown to Miss Watkins who may have expected to act as hostess. Afterwards she made a slight scene, and this Lockhart would not permit even from so valued a governess. The little storm blew over; but in August of that year, when Charlotte was in France with Miss Watkins, Lockhart wrote her his decision that it were better that 'you and she should not again spend the winter in your present relationship under this roof'. Everything must be done to

Anne, wife of John Murray II, by Elizabeth Rigby 1844

make the break easier for Miss Watkins; she would have excellent introductions if she wished to find another post; she must often come to visit Charlotte, but there must be no more exercise of authority.

Charlotte was already coming out in society under her father's care. At this particular dinner he nearly quarrelled with a fellow-guest, Turner the artist. Miss Rigby went to an exhibition of Turner's paintings and was impressed, finding that he 'does much as he likes with his brush, and if his likings are sometimes beyond our comprehension that is perhaps our fault. He can never be vulgar'.

Borrow, whose *Bible in Spain* Murray had published in 1843, and who was now writing *Lavengro*, came to dinner: 'a fine man, but a most disagreeable one; a character that would be most dangerous in rebellious times—one that would suffer or persecute to the last. His face is expressive of wrong-headed determination'.

Most important fellow-guest of all, though perhaps not realized as such at the moment, was Charles Eastlake, another artist, 'the Raphael of England' in Elizabeth's eyes which already may have begun to be partial.

She was taken to parties; one at the Misses Alexander, who were friends and neighbours of the Lockharts, in Sussex Place, Regent's Park, and of whom Lockhart writes with affectionate amusement in some of his letters. It was a musical party, Moscheles playing the piano, 'his taste stronger than his execution'.

And she called on other literary ladies. Agnes Strickland, historian of the Queens and Princesses of England, was 'the perfection of blues; she seems to think the most fortunate thing in life is to get a name!—but interesting'.

Lockhart would appear to have disliked this lady: 'Devil take Miss Agnes Strickland and all she-historians. I think I once met her many years ago. She called on Sir Walter, and my remembrance is of a rather handsome virago with the air of a Greenwich

E

booth tragedy Queen, but this may have been the sister'—so he once exploded in a letter, adding, however, that he thought her *Life of Mary of Modena* the best in the series of the Queens.

Maria Edgeworth, an old lady now with a great volume of work to her credit, was much less formidable. She sat sewing 'and I had the privilege of threading her needle'. Unfortunately no record was kept of the talk with either Miss Edgeworth or Miss Strickland.

Lord Shaftesbury took Miss Rigby to visit the female ward of Bedlam. Already treatment of the insane was improving, and she was impressed by the kindness of the attendants; but the atmosphere was infinitely sad: 'Even a sane cat, stretched on the sill in the sun, was delightful'.

And of course there was church-going. St. Paul's was not impressive: 'a great, bare building' and 'all the worse for not having been Roman Catholic', lacking the altars and chapels that might have focused some devotion. Sydney Smith preached on the text about the camel and the eye of a needle; a sermon 'which sounded more like a paper from *The Spectator*, terse, compact, sometimes swelling with poetry, sometimes warming into humour: one which every creature high and low could understand but none be improved by. . . . He himself looks, at first sight, like an old, pampered priest, but at second like the shrewd observer: one half of his face the stern moralist, the other the dry humorist.'

The company at No. 50 was brilliant; the fare probably excellent. Mrs. Murray's household guide might suitably be Mrs. Rundell, or she might consult the 'gastronomer in chief to the house of Murray and *The Quarterly*, Abraham Hayward, author of *The Art of Dining*, which had appeared as a series of articles in *The Quarterly*.

It was an age of dinners, now held in the evening, the old-fashioned afternoon hour having steadily advanced. Carlyle and Erasmus Darwin once estimated that in the West End of London there were 3,000 houses where any man of note would be welcomed as dinner-guest, during the season. Thackeray complained that one had the same dinner everywhere: soup, fish, saddle of mutton, boiled fowl, three or four entrées, 'confectioner's sweets, cheap champagne and hired waiters'. These were large and formal meals. The more Bohemian, impecunious or homely kind of hosts might provide a devil: as recommended and so well made by Mr. Micawber, and some toasted cheese. A couple giving four dinners for twenty guests each might spend £120; they would, of course, receive forty invitations in return.

Abraham Hayward might suggest a dinner of soup, turbot, venison, duckling with peas or chicken with asparagus, and 'a green apricot tart' which, if perfectly prepared, made 'a dinner fit for an emperor'. A plainer meal could be made interesting by one unusual dish, such as boiled duck or pheasant, kidney pudding or a partridge-pie with the birds sandwiched between beef-steaks.

A genial and comfortable world this, and it must have been as hard to leave it, for the rigours of a voyage to Reval again, as it was to say good-bye to the Murrays.

'Parted from dear John Murray with real regret', she wrote on the eve of her journey. This time, there was no peril of drowning, but the crossing was not agreeable:

'How impossible it is for the healthy to fancy sea-sickness, or for the sea-sick to fancy health.'

When free from sickness, she was bored:

'The humours of a cabin are but few; meals your greatest incident, and the stewardess your greatest annoyance.' Hers had asked if 'Russia was a nice place' which annoyed her as much as Carlyle's claim that Luther was a nice man. Miss Rigby had a feeling for words.

This visit to Reval, in company with a younger sister, lasted for three months, and she made fresh observations on Estonian manners, customs and oddities. There was the same love of titles as in Germany, a love so absurd that the untitled inscribed on their cards 'Sine titulo' in the manner of a later 'Failed B.A.'.

She found serfdom ruinous to both master and serfs; so many of these lived on the estate, bound to the land, but idle, paid nothing, contributing nothing, useless and enervated. In so vast a country there must be a gulf of ignorance between the centre and the edges. Laws could be distorted, even invented. In a story that demands treatment by Gogol to rival his *Dead Souls*, Miss Rigby told of a certain *mauvais sujet* in a remote province who, being in need of money told the people that the Emperor was demanding from them so many loads of snow. The people, credulous and submissive, grumbled only at the waste of man- and horse-power needed for transport. The *type* benevolently offered, for a sum of money, to arrange all that; the money was gladly contributed, 'and this was all he wanted'.

The Rigby ladies returned home via Stockholm where Elizabeth witnessed the coronation of the new King, and about a fortnight later described it in an article in *The Times*. They came back to Edinburgh, with a sense of home-coming, to take up the pleasant life of parties and church-going, and on Elizabeth's part, of writing. Lockhart was begging for further contributions:

'Bid your slave of Albemarle Street send you any books you want; he will be happy to obey his Queen Bess.'

So a package was dispatched, and in June 1845 an article on 'Lady Travellers' appeared in *The Quarterly*. It was warmly praised by Lockhart and, unexpectedly, by Croker:

'I scarcely think he ever said a word in favour of any article but his own', Lockhart told Miss Rigby.

The journalist in her was very active. Her Journal is so full of snappy descriptions that we realize her true scope would have been in a weekly *causerie*. *The Scotsman*, however, did not run to that, and many of its douce Presbyterian readers would not have relished some of her comments; her reference, for example, one Christmas Day to the church's being 'crammed with Presbyterians who coughed, sneezed, hemmed and blew their noses without ceasing. If they want any outpouring of the Spirit, why don't they hold prayer-meetings among themselves, instead of intruding into our Church on the very day which they have condemned in theirs?'

Even the spikiest Episcopalian may deplore a certain lack of charity here.

There are admirable vignettes and quotations; as this opinion of 'a bonny speech'. 'Aye, it's a bonny speech if ye no' tak' tent o' what he's saying'; which could be said, in Scotland at any time of all preachers in the wrong kirk and all politicians of the wrong party.

At one dinner party Lord Robertson convulsed the company with his 'sense, drollery, mimicry, wit, with lightning touches and unpremeditated combinations' which set 'the table roaring and the sideboard shaking'. (Does this refer to the footmen at the sideboard, trying to control their mirth?)

A party at Dean Ramsay's was even more delightful: the talk 'the best of all' and with 'the best of Christianity beaming through'. There was a reminiscence of Sir Walter Scott. Kemble was playing in Edinburgh, playing against a spiritless audience; then came a change. 'There's something in the house now,' he told the manager. Scott had entered the theatre, bringing his own responsive and infectious warmth. Another memory was of Scott's finding two children, their heads together, reading *Tales of a Grandfather*, and his exclaiming: 'That's the sort of popularity I like.'

Parties were fun, but 'how much more agreeable it is to receive friends than to visit them'—partly, no doubt, because one can then choose one's company, partly because of Edinburgh winds and weather: 'Very difficult to walk one way when your clothes are blowing another.'

At a concert, some of the singing was good but 'a man with black whiskers and a high voice is something disagreeable'. And she disliked the national instrument almost as much as she did the national kirk, quoting with approval a lady's remark that 'the sound of a bagpipe is like a magnified gnat'.

As for the kirk she was, in spite of her own occasional (and critical) attendance, shocked by the Queen's partiality for the Presbyterian way of worship. James II 'had not more offended against his coronation oath than Queen Victoria had done in going to a dissenting place of worship. What would they say to her attending Moorfields? And that's not nearly so derogatory to oath or principles as a Presbyterian kirk'.

In 1845 Miss Rigby visited Germany again: Cologne and Düsseldorf where John Murray had commissioned her to attend and describe an Exhibition of Modern German Art. Afterwards she wrote for *The Quarterly* on Cologne Cathedral, and on German Painting of which she thought poorly. In 1846 she was again in London, staying with the Murrays, renewing friendships, recording fresh impressions, good and bad. Best of all was that made by Charles Eastlake: 'most refined and amiable—quite the stamp of gentleman in the absence of all anxiety to show it'. Landseer too she admired with his 'head of power with that early grey hair which looks like the strength of youth and the wisdom of age mixed'.

Croker was 'singularly entertaining and singularly disagreeable, a handsome, disengenuous face, eyes catering all round for hearers to his tongue'. He was the most ferocious of all *The Quarterly* reviewers, preferring to flagellate rather than to praise. "Well, John, have you a Fool in the Forest for me?' he asked Lockhart; and Murray once exclaimed: 'Oh God, for a fool—not a woman—to throw into his cage!'

Murray had published *Eothen*, and the author, Kinglake, was at dinner: 'a heavy, shy-looking, plain little man, who stared sufficiently'—but who was much esteemed by his publisher. 'To say "Travels" to a Murray was like saying "Rats" to a terrier'—according to an historian of the house; John the Third pounced on travel-writers as eagerly as his father.

Among Miss Rigby's dislikes was Edward Lytton Bulwer, afterwards Bulwer Lytton, head of the 'silver fork' school of novelists and author also of *The Last Days of Pompeii*: 'a man with rather disagreeable manners, reminding me of some of the sub-heroes of his own books'. A good word 'sub-heroes', which could be widely applied!

Church-going took her to Westminster to hear Canon Words-worth, nephew of the poet, future Bishop of Lincoln, and father of a remarkable daughter, Elizabeth, who was to become Princi-pal of the first Oxford College for Women, Lady Margaret Hall. His sermon was 'dry and passionless, but earnest and ecclesiasti-cal'.

Murray was now at full flood, publishing history, biography, travel, new editions of the classics, and an illustrated Prayer Book. It was a book-buying, perhaps even a book-reading age. Country gentlemen were adding to their libraries, the clergy were, in the main, a scholarly body and some of them had means enough to indulge in new books; the newly rich merchants were aware that a library was an essential adjunct, if not a proof of gentility. Murray observed the custom of an annual sale, held after a dinner in the Albion Tavern in Fleet Street. After coffee, an auctioneer took the chair, put up the books for sale and took bids from the booksellers present. The price was already fixed, but discount was allowed to large purchasers.

Among the books of the day was *The Story of the Battle of Waterloo*, by George Robert Gleig, formerly an army chaplain, now chaplain to Chelsea Hospital; a friend of Lockhart, a contri-butor to *The Quarterly*, and well known as the author of a tale of the Peninsular War—*The Subaltern*. Thackeray was said to be awaiting his history of Waterloo with eagerness, in order to amplify the Waterloo chapter in *Vanity Fair*.

Mrs. Markham was bringing £1,400 a year in royalties to her publisher and to the author's husband—she herself being dead. Murray once suggested dropping the dialogue and conversation, but Mr. Penrose insisted that these 'introduced a tone of good breeding into the study of English history and were much appreciated by the middle classes'. This tone Murray himself so much admired that he tried to persuade Arthur Stanley and others

to 'turn themselves into Grecian and Roman Mrs. Markhams . . .
so lucid, so accurate, so free from all unpleasantness'—which
history so seldom is; but these gentlemen would not conform,
and so we lack any genteel conversations about ancient history.

The 1840's saw a revival, almost a turmoil within the
Church of England. The Oxford or Tractarian Movement,
dating from Keble's sermon in 1833 on The National Apostasy,
had effectively aroused the somnolent: some to devotion, others
to protest. The half-forgotten glories of Catholic worship,
teaching and discipline were discovered and brought forth; and
there was a storm of anti-ritualism. Some of the Tractarians
suffered persecution and endured bravely; others, unable to keep
their footing on the middle path, went over to the Roman obedience. *The Quarterly* published many articles on controversial
church matters; one by Croker, scandalized many readers including the editor, Lockhart, who was by no means unsympathetic with the Movement. One by Sewell spoke the mind of
the average High Churchman. Religion was the topic of the day.

Miss Rigby did not discuss these matters, but her tendency
was towards High Church views; and when, on her way north
again she visited a Carmelite Convent in Darlington she was
greatly pleased by the courtesy, cheerfulness and healthy appearance of the nuns. Walking steadily herself on the middle path she
looked benignly upon the Roman landscape on the one hand,
with distaste upon Presbyterianism on the other.

In August (1847) she was in Edinburgh once more, 'There is no
place like Edinburgh'; and attended the dinner given to celebrate
the completion of the Scott Monument in Princes Street, with the
erection therein of Steele's statue of Scott.

An article in *The Quarterly* on 'The Art of Dress' brought her a
compliment from Dean Ramsay who guessed the authorship. It
is probably to this article that she refers in an undated letter to
John Murray:

'I am very glad you had had discrimination enough to like that
article. It is just the thing for you to read with your present

prospects, and I think Menie should be very much obliged to me for this, and many other instances in which I have endeavoured to improve you.'

Menie was Marion Smith who, in 1847, became Mrs. John Murray. The marriage increased Miss Rigby's intimacy with No. 50 Albemarle Street:

'You will receive a treasure such as falls to few men's share,' she told the bridegroom; 'and we can trust you with it. I think it rather hard you did not request *me* to be your best man, but at all events I shall be there to see how you behave.'

Her activities in Edinburgh included 'making portraits and selling them for the Highlanders for whom there is to be a great Bazaar this week'.

The bazaar—for any and every kind of good cause—was approaching its zenith. Ladies of means, leisure and varying degrees of talent produced handiwork of every kind to be displayed on stalls and bought by a public that liked a well-furnished room.

Elizabeth witnessed the General Assembly of the Church of Scotland with a disparaging eye: 'Ugly, raw-boned men in rusty black clothes, with cotton umbrellas, by which one may always know a Scotch minister.'

She met Hans Andersen at a party: 'the Danish poet . . . a long, thin, fleshless, boneless man, wriggling and bending like a lizard, with a lantern-jawed, cadaverous visage. Simple and child-like, and simpletonish in manner'. One must wish she had drawn him with her pencil as well as her pen, and had sketched some of the unfortunate ministers.

An article on her German experiences appeared in *Fraser's Magazine*, and was praised by Lockhart without knowing it was hers. And in *The Quarterly*, in December 1848, came her most famous (or infamous) review: of *Jane Eyre*, in which she declared as if *ex cathedra*, that Currer Bell, the name under which Charlotte Brontë first hid herself, was certainly a man. This belief was fostered by Lockhart's gossip that Currer, Ellis and Acton Bell were three 'brothers of the weaving order in some Lancashire town'. The secret of Miss Rigby's authorship of this review was not generally discovered until 1892 when the famous Scots journalist and editor, William Robertson Nicoll, announced it in *The Bookman*.

This may be regarded as the climax of her journalism; the climax of her private life was reached soon afterwards. The friendship with Charles Eastlake, begun at Murray's, had deepened, and in January 1849 Elizabeth wrote to Menie Murray:

'I have obtained from Mr. E. a very ready assent to my informing Mr. Murray and you of this matter, and so you must consider yourselves now put in possession of it. He indeed seems pleased that I should desire it. . . . He owns himself very ignorant of all forms in such matters, not having committed such follies, I suppose, often before—as a proof of which he thinks that all the world might know without harm, which idea will have to be put out of him. He talks of coming for two days next month, and has some wild ideas connected with that visit which will have to be *nipped*. You will think me very composed, but I must *nip* that idea, too, for in reality I am sometimes, very often, very disturbed. The slightness of our acquaintance still comes over me most harassingly sometimes. I see nothing but the leaving of all I hold most dear, and dear *Edinburgh* into the bargain, for a stranger I hardly know the look of yet—for I have quite forgotten what he is like!

'I am not going to trifle with him, my dearest, nor to be unreasonable, but I must be allowed to feel a trifle *variable* though I may not act so. He is improving in the *writing* department, but still terrifies me with the piece of perfection he expects. Altogether there never was an old bachelor committed such a wilful bit of imprudence before. May he live to repent it!'

It was a natural attitude towards a late marriage, if a little over-protesting and slightly coy, in a woman who had made herself a career of a sort at once unusual and entirely proper, and who enjoyed a rich family and social life of her own.

She wrote of her future husband:

'He has always been the object of my particular admiration for his gentle, refined manner and cultivated conversation. I have always met him with unfeigned pleasure. I believe him to be the right man for me, and am more and more happy in the thought of spending my life with him.'

They were indeed a well-matched pair. Eastlake was sixteen years her senior; born in 1793, the son of an Admiralty agent in Plymouth where he attended the grammar school, and had drawing lessons from Samuel Prout. In everything he was, as his wife was to record of him in her Memoir, 'conscientious, painstaking and ambitious . . . a quiet and studious boy, and determined to do well whatever he undertook'. He loved poetry and music as well as his own art of drawing and painting. From his grammar school he went to Charterhouse, but soon exchanged that for the Royal Academy Schools, having resolved to be an historical painter. There his fellow-townsman, Benjamin Haydon, took him under his wing.

There can never have been an art student of less (so-called) artistic temperament or Bohemian ways. Young Eastlake worked steadily and methodically, and every day read the classics for two hours until he could enjoy Homer and Virgil without a dictionary. This he held necessary for his vocation as an historical painter. From the first he was successful in winning commissions.

In 1814 and again in 1815 he went to France, during the temporary peace, and exile of Napoleon. On the eve of the Hundred Days he left Paris—at the same time as its King Louis XVIII; but when Waterloo was fought and Napoleon again captive, he made high artistic profit. The *Bellerophon* taking Napoleon to St. Helena put into Plymouth Sound, and young Eastlake sailed round her making sketches of the Emperor. For the subsequent portrait and portrait-group he received £1,000. This took him to Italy where he spent the next fourteen years, varied by a tour of Greece. Most of the time he lived happily and fruitfully in Rome, consorting with famous Anglo-Romans: the

Misses Berry, Samuel Rogers, Captain and Mrs. Graham (she was, by her second marriage, Lady Callcott), the author of *Little Arthur's History of England*, Thomas Moore, Sir Humphry Davy, and his own fellow-artists Etty and Sir Thomas Lawrence. It was a period of immense industry as well as of stimulus. He did not forget his ambition to be an historical painter, but he did a great deal of landscape painting, especially of landscape with figures, which was to prove extremely popular in England: a foreign scene was so picturesque, and foreign types so fascinating. His pictures of bandits appealed to respectable and wealthy English citizens, as did his subject-paintings: *Pilgrims Approaching Rome, Byron's Dream*, and others being greatly admired. Art was becoming literary.

Returning to London in 1830 he found himself increasingly busy and successful. He was much in demand for portraits of ladies in fancy dress, and his Biblical paintings pleased the public taste: his famous *Hagar and Ishmael, Christ Blessing Little Children,* and *Christ Weeping Over Jerusalem*. He became an Associate of the Royal Academy, and in 1842 was appointed Librarian; he was also Secretary to the Fine Arts Commission set up to supervise the decoration of the Houses of Parliament. This brought him into touch with Royalty, and he became chief, if unofficial adviser to the Prince Consort and to the Government on matters of art. In 1848 he published *Contributions to the Literature of the Fine Arts*.

It was altogether a most cultivated, well-esteemed and well-established bridegroom who, on 10th April, 1849, led Elizabeth Rigby to the altar of St. John's Church in Edinburgh, to be blessed by Dean Ramsay. The middle-aged and most congenial pair took up house in London, in Fitzroy Square, and a new chapter began for Elizabeth, one of even happier experience than her contented spinsterhood.

Sir Charles Eastlake, P.R.A., by John Partridge

VII

THE QUARTERLY. MISS RIGBY WRITES

I

ON 'LADY TRAVELLERS'

THE article in June 1845 on 'Lady Travellers' dealt with a number of volumes of travel, by women, all of them amateurs in writing, of varying degrees of talent; the scene ranging from Mexico to Madras, from New South Wales to Vienna, from Portugal to Palestine. The survey in general was most favourable.

Women, in Miss Rigby's opinion, were expected to write good travel books, for women had an eye for detail and a sense of news. Feminine defects in education were no hindrance: 'If the gentleman knows more of ancient history and ancient languages, the lady knows more of human nature and modern languages.' There is in this, as in the later article on 'Dress', a curious pretence or pose of masculinity on the part of the reviewer; a tone of would-be masculine gallantry towards 'the ladies' and to 'that power of observation which, so long as it remains at home counting canvas stitches by the fireside, we are apt to consider no shrewder than our own, but when once removed from the familiar scene and returned to us in the shape of books, seldom fails to prove its superiority'.

Travel books had much in common with letters; the same gifts were needed to make either of these delightful reading:

'Who, for instance, has not turned from the slapdash scrawl of your male correspondent—with excuses at the beginning and haste at the end . . . to the well-filled sheet of your female friend, with plenty of time bestowed and no paper wasted, and over-flowing with those close and lively details which show not only that observing eyes have been at work, but one pair of bright eyes in particular? Or who does not know the difference between their books—especially their books of travel—the gentleman's either dull and matter-of-fact or offhand and superficial, and the lady's all ease, animation, vivacity, with the tact to dwell upon what you most want to know, and the sense to pass over what she does not know herself.'

Travel writing was, to her mind, the most revealing form of writing: 'We form a clearer idea of the writer of the most un-pretending book of travels than we do of her who gives us the most striking work of imagination. The undercurrent of personality, however little obtruded to sight, is sure to be genuine.

The article did not deal with the professional woman of letters like Mrs. Trollope, whose book on America had caused no small stir. The authors reviewed were all cultivated women of the world, observant and accomplished; not in the strict sense literary. Two foreign books were commended: *Life in Mexico* by Madame Calderon de la Barca, and *Orientale Briefe* by Ida, Countess Hahn-Hahn; but this *genre* was peculiarly the domain of Englishwomen, and England was richer than any other country in women who were 'well-read, solid-thinking, early-rising, sketch-loving, light-footed, trim-waisted, straw-hatted . . . educated with the re-finement of the highest and the usefulness of the lowest classes'. A woman like that was an 'all-sufficient companion to her hus-band, and an all-sufficient lady's maid to herself'.

This superiority revealed the defects of other nations: 'The German ladies, with all their virtues, are not supposed to excel in rapid observation or lively delineation. Inward experiences and not outward impressions are their *forte*—the eyes of their souls are brighter than those of their bodies' (and who wants to look into the eyes of a soul?). Miss Rigby made one exception: the Countess Hahn-Hahn whose *Oriental Letters* she had enjoyed.

The Frenchwoman, on the other hand, had both eyes and tongue 'of the most lively description' and was 'a brilliant ob-server' but had one slight fault: 'She cannot spell.' (Surely a trivial objection! A proof-reader could attend to that!)

The Englishwoman had qualities of both mind and heart, of both physical and mental training. There was 'so much of Ruth in her heart' that 'wherever she goes a little patch of household comfort grows beneath her feet, wherever there is room for rational tastes, orderly habits and gentle charities . . . there we find the Englishwomen creating an atmosphere of virtuous happiness around her . . . There is no part of the world, however remote, from which she does not send forth a voice of cheerful intelligence.'

After a brief reference to an 'older work of great value and attraction'—Lady Callcott's *Residence in the Brazils*, and, either in self-advertisement or disguise, to her own *Letters From the Baltic,* she began a detailed discussion of the books under review. That on New South Wales, by Mrs. Meredith, was in part natural history, and in part a lively comment on the varieties, oddities, and snobberies of 'the *beau monde* of Sydney'.

From Australia the reader passed to Egypt, with Mrs. Poole's *Englishwoman in Egypt.* The author was sister to Edward Lane the famous traveller and Egyptologist, and her book was intended to be 'an humble helpmate to his well-known *Modern Egyptians*'. She had herself 'no learning and not much sentiment' but she had modesty and a 'most artless simplicity'; and was apparently a gentle and tactful woman, who adapted herself very well to the strange society of Egypt, noting and recording impressions, giving such details of domestic life in the harem as every woman would want to read.

Her book was entertaining; and a book of Indian travel— *Letters from Madras By a Lady* was equally delightful. Then came the turn of Madame Calderon de la Barca's *Life in Mexico.* That lady was regarded as a foreigner, and was indeed Spanish by her marriage to a Spanish diplomat (a collateral descendant of the poet Calderon); but she was by birth Scottish, an Erskine, brought up in Edinburgh; then instead of marrying an advocate and settling down in the society that welcomed Miss Rigby she had gone with her family to New York, and there met her future husband. On her marriage she had become a Catholic. From Presbyterianism to Popery was not a downward step, but the mixture was bad, in Miss Rigby's eyes, and was partly the reason for 'the very unEnglish nature of her writing'.

It was impossible not to admire her book—which indeed is still fascinating, truly part of travel literature, and even in this review stands out from its fellows as a work of art.

Miss Rigby admitted her liveliness, intelligence and spirit; but she was not captivated, and one becomes aware of a conflict in her mind between prejudice and objective admiration. As a woman of letters herself, she could not deny the brilliance of Madame Calderon's writing, but she read without sympathy:

'We feel that it is not only tropical life we are reading, but, with the exception of an occasional trait of Scottish shrewdness and, we must say it, of Yankee vulgarity, a tropical mind that is addressing us.' With all her love of Scotland, Miss Rigby could not comprehend how often and how deeply the Scots mind has been captivated by the Latin, the northern temper by the southern and exotic.

In her eyes, too, Madame Calderon was rendered unfeminine by two tastes, natural to the Spanish lady, but not well regarded in Edinburgh: she was an amateur of bull-fighting and she smoked cigarettes. A Scotswoman become Spanish was like an Englishman Italianate. Miss Rigby was puzzled: 'The reel and the bolero may be nearer allied than we imagined'—as indeed they are.

She was startled by 'a Spanish indifference to bloodshed, a Spanish enthusiasm for bullfights, a Murillo glow of colour, a Cervantes touch of humour, a gentle defence of the *cigarito*, and a hard hit at John Knox'—which surely did not displease this journalist who had herself so vituperated Knox's successors in the kirks of Edinburgh!

The accounts of bull-fights might have been striking in a masculine author, such as Basil Hall; in a lady they were shocking, and Miss Rigby preferred the attitude of an Englishwoman in

Portugal, Mrs. Romer, who in her account of *The Rhone, The Douro and The Guadalquivir* confessed to having covered her eyes in terror and pity at the beginning of the fight, and presently to have fled from the arena in horror. What was therefore undescribed was, to Miss Rigby's mind, more vivid than the expert but unbecoming description by Madame Calderon.

She could be shocked by lapses from her own standards of taste and feeling, but she could also be mildly satirical about books and authors whose excellent morals were not matched by literary skill, though their background was aristocratic. They travelled in luxury, mellowing the rigours of the East with 'Medical men and air-cushions, and ladies' maids and canteens. and portable tents and Douro chairs and daguerrotypes'. Their assumption of aristocratic standards could be amusing and their style artless. On the whole, however, these well-bred records of travel did credit to their authors, revealing 'that spirit of good sense, good feeling and good principle which we have ever fondly attributed to the highest ranks of our Englishwoman'.

Lady Francis Egerton and the Honourable Mrs. Dawson Damer might be a little superficial in describing the Holy Land, overinclined to inform the reader that this Eastern lady or that was very like Lady A. F. or Lady F. E. But they wrote with good feeling. Mrs. Dawson Damer especially took the reader 'to the innermost boudoir of modern fashion. But though the light is stifled with draperies, and the air heavy with perfumes, and every step impeded with prettinesses and uselessnesses and nonsenses without end, yet a stream of pure feeling plays through and genuine mirth is heard, and genuine kindness felt'.

Lady Grosvenor's account of her yachting experiences was given 'without fuss or finery' and was altogether a 'sensible, healthy and well-written work'—by one whose mind 'has evidently so much fresh air to it' that the reader could see 'the healthy English home she has left'.

Most eminent and most formidable of the great ladies was Harriet Vane, Marchioness of Londonderry whose sense of her own importance might account for 'the very decided tone we observe in her Ladyship's style of writing'—about her *Visit to the Courts of Vienna and Constantinople*—'even as to matters which usually pass for trifles. But Lady Londonderry feels and shows that to those who have a great public object at heart, there are no such things as trifles'.

The humorous eye is turned upon the Marchioness, and the *résumé* of her book is written with an irony not unworthy of Jane Austen.

'Her ladyship dwells with amiable minuteness upon the eagerness of various illustrious individuals to do them her [husband and herself] honour, but is equally anxious we should be informed of all occasions when personages of similar dignity manifested inferior discernment. In this respect indeed the Marquis and Marchioness seem to have been particularly tried'—by Royal forgetfulness and Royal snubs; and the Marchioness in particular by the shock her appearance in an elegant but *décolletée* court dress gave to the Moslems who ran away from her. 'To those not acquainted with the secret springs of policy which sustained the noble Marchioness, the whole affair might appear absurd and even derogatory'; as might also her presentation to the Bey of Tangiers when she appeared in her 'travelling gown and old, straw poke bonnet, *with her jewels over them*'. Miss Rigby concluded that whatever else might be thought of this work of 'our grandest insular specimen' it must be found 'rich in amusement' and worthy to be 'printed in satin and inlaid with as many crests and coronets as Debrett'.

Finally, she declared, in general retrospect: 'It is not for any endowments of intellect, either natural or acquired, that we care to prove the Englishwoman's superiority over all her foreign sisters, but for that soundness of principle and healthiness of heart without which the most brilliant of women's books, like the most brilliant woman herself, never fails to leave the sense of something wanted—a something better than all she has besides.'

II

ON 'DRESS'

Probably the most frivolous article to appear in the august pages of *The Quarterly*, at least in Victorian days, was Miss Rigby's, in March 1847, on *The Art of Dress*, with special reference to three books on the subject: *British Costume*, by J. R. Planché; *Costume in England*, by F. W. Fairholt; and *The Book of Costume and Annals of Fashion*, by a Lady of Rank.

The books are long forgotten, the commentary is still fresh and lively, and with certain changes and omissions might appear today in a woman's magazine of the superior kind and with space to spare. Again a masculine disguise was assumed, and was no more concealing than a man's coat worn over a full-skirted gown, with a man's hat pulled over feminine curls and ringlets. Again there is a somewhat forced gallantry towards 'the ladies', an occasional reference to 'us men'; but the tone is so feminine that a much less astute reader than Dean Ramsay would guess the sex if not the name of the author.

She begins with a lively attack on contemporary male dress as 'a mysterious combination of the inconvenient and the un-picturesque . . . hot in summer, cold in winter, useless for keeping off rain or sun, stiff but not plain, bare without being simple, not durable, and not cheap. . . . Not a single article is left in his ward-robe' with which wretched man 'can even make what is called an impression—a conquest is out of the question'. A good wife must dress for two, in order to reflect some glory upon her drab spouse.

The Victorian man was wearing dark clothes; stove-pipe trousers, long coat, high hat, linen immaculate but severe. The grandeur of the eighteenth century, the elegance of the Regency were banished. The only hint of splendour now lay in a waist-coat, and even there was deprecated as frivolous or flashy, while a display of jewellery was downright vulgar. To carry an umbrella was more common and more practical than to understand 'the nice conduct of a clouded cane'.

Women's dress, in the 1840's was still graceful; future decades held the exaggeration of the crinoline and the bustle, the ostentatious richness of material, elaboration of trimming, the crude and ill-matched colours. There was a good line about feminine styles: a natural waist, long, but not heavy skirts, a plain bodice, *décolletée* for evening, with pretty collar or fichu for day wear. Hats and bonnets were both worn, the bonnet small and showing the hair. If the delicate grace of an earlier decade was lost—that of the modes revived in later years by Kate Greenaway—the vogue of the moment still had elegance without the crude elaboration of what is usually meant by Victorian fashions.

For Elizabeth, as for any contemporary writer on fashion, dress was 'a sort of personal glossary' or as we might say, an expression of personality. 'Every woman walks about with a placard in which her leading qualities are advertised.'

Fashion should be treated with courtesy and followed with discretion. There was always the woman who, in terror of being out of the vogue, rushed to its most fantastic heights; she wore exaggerated styles, violent colours, extravagances of every kind—all with a dejected air, as if dismayed by finding herself in such garb. A foolish type this, but the despiser of fashion was even worse. She was aggressively plain, almost masculine in style, making the least and worst of herself as a woman, obviously strong-minded and coarse of texture, 'probably a radical, certainly a dissenter, very likely somewhat of a sceptic' (and what worse could be said of anyone?).

To be richly but dowdily dressed, in costly but ill-made silks with an unbecoming hat or bonnet, showed the Puritan or Evangelical. This type was not vulgar, like her predecessor, because she was invariably neat, and 'not otherwise than a lady, though there is not the slightest wish evident of being thought one'. She might be recognized by her 'cold, mild eye and headachy complexion'.

But the lady with a true sense of dress—delightful creature—adopted and adapted the vogue with exquisite tact, following her own line within the limits of fashion; she wore beautiful dresses that had the air of Paris but were, as often as not, made at home from material bought in the local shop. They might often be cheap, they were always pretty, becoming and in every way right. She knew, this charming lady, 'the three grand unities of dress—her own station, her own age, and her own points. And no woman can dress well who does not'. Except that no journalist today dare mention the matter of rank or station, this ruling could be proclaimed in any fashion magazine.

This lady was likely to be not only perfectly dressed and charming in looks and manner, but good-tempered, intelligent, sensible, well-informed; in short 'a complete lady'.

To affect indifference towards dress was detestable; an interest in fashion was natural and healthy. 'The final cause of dress' was 'an instinct implanted in man and exercised by woman wholly for his good'. A woman 'dresses herself to please him, and he dresses her to please himself'.

Coming down to details, Miss Rigby liked the current styles: the long skirts were graceful and so were flounces, if the material were light, and if 'the lady has an outline but no mass' (and not a 'demned outline' like Mr. Mantalini's Countess). She did not care for the newly modish shawl unless it were worn with a Spanish grace, not put on square and sensible as too often it was. The line of a shawl seen from the back could be depressing. Much more elegant was the black silk scarf, also in vogue; this gave a finished look to any dress: 'it carries an air of self-respect with it which is in itself a protection'.

One sees her own tall figure dressed in a good silk gown with a black silk scarf gracefully disposed over her shoulders, walking along Princes Street, bowing to acquaintances, pausing to speak to the Dean and his lady, glancing at the Scott Monument, turning into Blackwood's to look at some new books. On her head she might wear a small bonnet, or a plain straw hat. This form of headgear she warmly approved; the hats of the moment did not much attract her but the plain straw was always suitable and universally becoming: 'It refines the homeliest and composes the wildest—it gives the coquettish young lady a little dash of demureness, and the demure one a slight touch of coquetry'. Never vulgar, it made the perfect accompaniment to the black silk scarf.

It was a mistake for all classes, let alone all ages to try to dress alike. This was not mere snobbery. Certain styles demanded delicate materials or rich silks, and a graceful figure and carriage to wear them properly. The peasant woman 'ought not to remind us of a lady at all'. Miss Rigby did not mention the fat dowager, the horse-faced lady of rank, the worthy but plain-headed gentlewoman upon whom no finery could ever appear elegant. But she rightly deplored the passing of some garments that were kind to old faces: the white goffered cap, with ruffles or neckerchief seen in portraits. In Scotland, however, she must have seen many an old wife wearing her white mutch with dignity. The bonny red cloak that once wrapped so many countrywomen going to the kirk was making way for the Paisley shawl—which one would expect to have pleased an artist's eye with its subdued richness of colour and pattern. In justice to Miss Rigby's dress snobbery it must be remembered that it was not easy, in those days before the invention of the sewing-machine, to copy a fine silk gown effectively in some cheap material. The poor were well-advised to be simple in dress.

III

ON 'JANE EYRE'

In this review Miss Rigby passes from geniality to acerbity.

Rejecting the scandalous gossip that this was a former governess of Thackeray's daughters (some added his own mistress) portrayed by him in Becky Sharp and now taking her revenge, she

announced decisively that Currer Bell was masculine in fact as
in name: a man 'who, with great mental powers combines a
total ignorance of the habits of society, a great coarseness of taste,
and a heathenish doctrine of religion'.

This last charge is difficult to understand; for poor Jane is
driven by conscience and religious scruples to flee from her
adored Rochester into poverty and insecurity rather than live
with him in luxury and sin; and when she returns to him she
finds a reformed and religious character. 'Coarseness of taste' is
also difficult to detect; unless, to Miss Rigby, outspoken mutual
passion was coarse.

The main argument for masculine authorship, however, lay
in domestic and personal details:

'No woman ... trusses game and garnishes dessert-dishes with
the same hand'—referring to Jane's account of the preparations at
Thornton Hall for the house-party, when she was drawn into
willing service by Mrs. Fairfax, and was constantly in and out of
kitchen and still-room 'helping or hindering her and the cook',
learning to truss game and prepare desserts. For most readers this
is a homely and realistic passage, obviously written by a domestic
woman as Charlotte Brontë undoubtedly was. Jane's various
activities are telescoped for brevity, not through ignorance.
Charlotte might be Celtic by blood, and show it in her poetry and
passion; but by upbringing she was as good a Yorkshirewoman
as ever baked light bread and kept a house of exquisite cleanness.
In one of the later chapters Jane helps her cousins' housekeeper,
Hannah, to clean and re-furnish the old parsonage, and make
puddings and pies for Christmas; she works with such zest and
skill as to win a compliment from her austere companion. Like
many a reviewer of her own day and after, Miss Rigby saw what
she wanted to see, and adjusted illustrations to fit her theory.

Jane's notions of dress shocked her:

'No woman attires another in such fancy dress' as Miss Ingram's morning-gown of sky-blue crape. Agreed; and sky-blue
anything was a disaster for a lady of complexion 'as dark as a

Spaniard'. But Jane's sense of finery in both dress and furniture
was adolescent—though entirely feminine; she (like her creator)
was starved of colour and richness. She was like a schoolgirl who
plans creations as different as possible from the school blue serge
or grey flannel. There was a dual personality in both Jane and
Charlotte: a rather endearing adolescent who furnished the
dining-room at Thornton Hall with purple carpet, chairs and
curtains, with stained-glass window, and the drawing-room in a
blending of 'fire and snow'—white carpet, red chairs and otto-
mans, glittering chandelier and gleaming pier-glass; who
watched the ladies of the house-party enter the room in snowy
draperies or changing silks, with pearls and diamonds. The other
person in them was a severe little Puritan whose own idea of
splendour was a pale-grey silk gown and a little pearl brooch;
who in choosing her trousseau rejected pinks and blues, and
accepted only black and grey.

Jane's own sober dress could not be found unladylike; but 'no
lady when roused in the night' as she was by the yells of the
maniac, 'would think of hurrying on a "frock"'. She would
assume 'a garment more convenient for such occasions and more
becoming'. But Jane, with her meagre salary at Lowood had
probably been unable to afford herself a dressing-gown; and
even if she did possess one, she would have been of little use, that
night, trailing around like the others in a voluminous white
wrapper. Her black frock and list slippers made her practically
invisible and inaudible, and her wearing them showed great
presence of mind.

The ignorance of society was a true charge and still provides
unintended comic relief. Jane's or Charlotte's most ardent
admirers cannot easily accept those house-party scenes; and would
agree that Miss Ingram and her mother 'talk like *parvenues* trying
to show off'. Miss Ingram's: 'Am I right, my Baroness Ingram
of Ingram Park?' and her address to the footman, 'Cease that
chatter, blockhead, and do my bidding', are among the immortal
absurdities of fiction. Such ignorance was natural in an author

who was almost a recluse, with no knowledge of the world beyond her own county; it was hardly a moral flaw, a sign of coarseness, or a proof of masculinity.

These, however, were minor blots; the fundamental fault of the book, in Miss Rigby's eyes, was its immorality. Jane herself was condemned as base and vulgar: 'an uninteresting, sententious, pedantic thing' who 'in every word she utters offends us' by her 'pedantry, stupidity and gross vulgarity'; who shows 'an unregenerate and undisciplined spirit' of pride and rebellion, devoid of Christian grace. Miss Rigby would seem, for the moment, to have borrowed the pen of Mrs. Sherwood. We may be certain that that lady spoke in no more severe reprobation than this of a novel she cannot have approved—if indeed she read it.

'It is a very remarkable book; we have no remembrance of another combining such genuine power with such horrid taste'. Mr. Rochester was a deplorable hero, seeking 'deliberately and secretly to violate the laws of God and man'; but the reviewer believed rightly that 'half our lady readers are enchanted with him'.

In youth, we are; in maturity most of us realize how essentially Mr. Rochester is the creation of a feminine imagination. In masculine eyes he is, if taken seriously, a good deal of a cad; if not, then a comic character. Only a woman, and an unsophisticated one, would invest him with Byronic glamour, be thrilled by his saturnine looks, a *beau laid* if ever there was one, and by his language spiced with oaths that the Victorian gentleman was already ceasing to utter in the presence of ladies. Mr. Rochester is a schoolgirl's dream of dangerous masculinity.

In Miss Rigby's cold eyes he was base; and Jane was worse: 'one whom we should not care for as an acquaintance, whom we should not seek as a friend, whom we should not desire as a relation, and whom we should scrupulously avoid as a governess'.

Even in those days when authors were liable to be figuratively hanged, drawn and quartered in public, this was carrying out the sentence with the utmost rigour of the law. The author of *Jane*

Eyre was judged guilty of 'that highest moral offence a novel writer can commit, that of making an unworthy character interesting in the eyes of the reader'.

Jane was shocking in her unveiled passion, especially in the orchard scene. Even her struggle with the agony of lawless love, and her victory were not commended. Her fortitude was pagan; there was no Christian grace in her and her autobiography was 'pre-eminently an anti-Christian composition' full of 'a proud and perpetual assertion of the rights of man, for which we can find no authority either in God's Word or in God's Providence'. It was the spirit of Chartism, and nothing worse could be said; though in her mind Miss Rigby may have suspected Currer Bell of being no better than a Presbyterian.

So she reached her climax—the head of Currer Bell set up on Tower Hill after the execution!

'If we ascribe the book to a woman at all, we have no alternative but to ascribe it to one who has, for some sufficient reason, long forfeited the society of her own sex.'

The irony of it is that had Elizabeth known the facts of Charlotte Brontë's austere, secluded life, had she met that indomitable gentlewoman she must have recognized in her a cultivated mind, a true breeding, a Christian fortitude. A friendship between them would have been of great enrichment to Charlotte in the last lonely years between the deaths of Emily and Anne, and her own brief marriage.

It is a psychological problem, this outbreak of acerbity, almost of savagery in a woman of warm and wide sympathies, a woman of the world by no means prim or spinsterish, at ease in masculine company. There seems to have been an infection in the very air of the world of letters, prevalent for many years, infecting nearly every writer who undertook the task of criticism. Croker was unique in degree of cruelty but not in kind; Lockhart's attack on Keats was still remembered. Murray and Lockhart would not, if they could help it, deliver a female writer to Croker, for no idea of chivalry or approach to gentleness would enter his arrogant head. But here was a gentlewoman rivalling both Lockhart and Croker in ferocity, with her own feminine talent for getting under the skin of her victim.

And one of the oddities, or apparent inconsistencies in this article is Miss Rigby's admiration for Becky Sharp; for she was reviewing *Vanity Fair* along with *Jane Eyre*—the two novels bound, as it were, together by the occupation of both heroines. Her attitude to Becky is one of artistic delight, unclouded by moral disapproval. Far from being shocked by that adroit little sinner she was amused, even captivated by her, and saw her as a creature distinct from ordinary women. In this she was right; to deplore Becky's lack of moral rectitude is like deploring a certain lack of domestic stability in Undine.

'Considering Becky in her human character we know of none which so thoroughly satisfies our *beau idéal* of feminine wickedness, with so slight a shock to our feelings and proprieties' as she, for she is a creature of another world, and not 'one of us'.

Becky and Jane 'both have an elfish kind of nature, with which they divine the secrets of other hearts and conceal those of their own'. Rochester was attracted by this very elfish quality in Jane; but there was little concealment on her part of her feelings. Becky truly had all the elfin coldness: 'Wickedness and goodness, unless coupled with strength, were alike worthless to her' and her own goodness went only as far as 'good temper and . . . shrewd sense'; so that the reader should thank her for showing 'what they are both worth'. She was not Christian in either thought or act, but then one does not expect an elf to be a Christian.

'The great charm, therefore, and comfort of Becky is that we may study her without any compunctions', and in the end, be grateful to her for discovering the worth of Dobbin whom the imbecile Amelia ignores: 'Dobbin sheds a halo over all the long-necked, loose-jointed, Scotch-looking gentlemen of our acquaintance. Flat feet and flap ears seem henceforth incompatible with evil' however depressing in themselves.

It is 'curiouser and curiouser'. Mr. Thackeray could ride off on a stolen horse, while Currer Bell might not look over the fence. In mid-review Miss Rigby changes from a humorous, ironic and perceptive woman of letters to a shocked, vituperative spinster. Even now, the reader is left with a sense of bewilderment, almost of revulsion, as if witnessing a change of personality.

Her publishers tried to withhold the review from Charlotte Brontë; but that stern spirit would not accept the merciful concealment. She demanded that *The Quarterly* be sent her; and received the blows as her Helen Burns had taken the whipping administered by Miss Scatcherd at Lowood, without an apparent tear:

'Untoward circumstances come to me, I think, less painfully than pleasant ones would just now. The lash of *The Quarterly*, however severely applied, cannot sting—as its praise probably would not elate me. Currer Bell feels a sorrowful independence of reviews and reviewers; their approbation might indeed fall like a sorrowful weight on his heart, but their censure has no bitterness for him.' So she wrote to her discoverer and adviser, Mr. Williams of Smith and Elder; and again:

'I read *The Quarterly* without a pang, except that I thought there were some sentences disgraceful to the critic. He seems anxious to let it be understood that he is a person well acquainted with the habits of the upper classes. Be this as it may, I am afraid he is no gentleman.'

What might (or must?) have been the cruellest lash of the whip —'if by a woman . . .' she treated with contempt:

'To such critics I would say: "To you I am neither man nor woman, I come before you as an author only",' which was sound defence.

But the lash must have stung. She kept the review from her father. Her sisters were dead: 'so remote from earth, so safe from its turmoils, I can bear it better'.

She thought of referring to the article in a preface to *Shirley* which was then going to press:

'I must speak . . . just one little word. You once, I remember, said that review was written by a lady—Miss Rigby. Are you sure of this?

'Give no hint of my intention of discoursing a little with *The Quarterly*. It would look too important to speak of it beforehand. All plans are best conceived and executed without noise.'

Mr. Williams, however, counselled her against even that one little word. *Shirley* appeared without preface. Mrs. Gaskell says that Charlotte took no more notice 'of the article than to place a few sentences out of it in the mouth of a hard and vulgar woman in Shirley, where they are so much in character that few have recognized them as a quotation'.

This refers, probably, to Mrs. Hardman of whom Mrs. Pryor tells Caroline Helstone in a long, intimate conversation. She is recalling the misery of her own first post as a governess in the Hardman family, when her employer, far from giving her any help, sympathy or reasonable courtesy, bade her overcome her 'ungodly discontent' and cease 'murmuring against God's appointment': the very reproaches that Miss Rigby made against Jane.

The strangeness of the attack on *Jane Eyre* is enhanced by the conclusion of the article, in which Miss Rigby deals most sympathetically with a Report of the Governesses' Benevolent Institution: that recent and most necessary foundation for the aiding of governesses grown old or ill, or thrown out of work, with no savings from their meagre salaries, no family to offer a refuge, no watchful benevolence on the part of former pupils or employers.

Miss Rigby wrote of them with understanding and compassion. They were often incompetent, through defective education, often the victims of paternal extravagance or carelessness; left without means, prohibited by convention and by their own notions of gentility from entering domestic service (and indeed incompetent in that way) they drifted into the schoolrooms of countless homes, and when their pupils were 'finished', come out in society, married, they drifted out again.

'There is no other class which so cruelly requires its members to be in birth, mind and manners above their station, in order to fit them for their station.' The governess was often kept apart from her employers, a little beneath them; admitted to the dining-room when there was no company, banished to the schoolroom when there were guests; seen, occasionally, in an obscure corner of the drawing-room. She was above the servants; in theory a lady; unable or unwilling to mix with them. The servants for their part were at liberty to despise her; and a housekeeper was a person of infinitely more authority in the house than the poor governess.

There were exceptional governesses; women of solid education and real culture, loved by their pupils and employers, who remained as friends long after the regimen of the schoolroom ended. Charlotte Lockhart's Miss Watkins would appear to have been of this kind; and although Lockhart had to dismiss her as governess, the friendship between her and Charlotte endured, and it is unlikely that she knew penury. A generation earlier Charlotte's mother Sophia, and Anne Scott had known a beloved governess, Miss Miller. Miss Rigby's picture was sombre, but it was true of far too many unfortunate gentlewomen.

There might be no active ill-treatment, no open insolence, but for most governesses there were many pricks and snubs:

'She must be a saint or no woman at all who can rise above perpetual little water-dropping trials.'

There were more governesses than women of any other class in the lunatic asylums: 'Wounded vanity is the rock on which most wounded minds go to pieces.' And even if well-treated by employers and respectfully by servants, there was always loneliness.

'Man cannot live by the head alone, far less woman.' To have, in the Victorian phrase 'resources in oneself' was not a panacea. 'A governess has no equals and therefore can have no sympathy.' Her pupils might love her but they could rarely be her enduring friends; she must, to all intents and purposes, live alone even in a thronging household.

This description, if one-sided, ignoring almost completely the happy relations that could and did exist in some families, was excellent propaganda for the down-trodden class; a moving plea for the Institution that tried to help them—with money, with shelter, with some approach to companionship; there was the nucleus of a Guild in it. The Institution appealed for funds to establish annuities for old governesses. There was a savings bank for whatever anyone could spare from her tiny salary. The most highly qualified governess in the best family was unlikely to be paid more than £120 a year. (Jane Eyre thought herself more than passing rich on £30.) The Institution tried also to provide for illness, and to make a home for the old.

It was the most admirable of good causes, and Miss Rigby pleaded it well. If only she had known she might have drawn a most poignant illustration from the experience of the author of *Jane Eyre*: Charlotte Brontë's bitter memory of the little boy who exclaimed at lunch, one day, 'I love 'oo, Miss Brontë', only to be reproved by his mother: 'Love the governess, my dear!'

She could have quoted from the discussion of governesses by Mr. Rochester's guests, in the presence of Jane herself; and she might have shown Jane as a pattern of competence. Neither Jane nor Becky could perhaps be chosen to illustrate the haplessness of the profession. Jane was welcomed with motherly kindness by Mrs. Fairfax, treated with complete respect by Leah and the other servants, loved by her pupil Adèle. It was only the complication of falling in love with her employer that made her miserable and the most benevolent Institution cannot prevent that.

As for Becky—neither master nor servant, pupil nor parent could daunt her. She is, admittedly, unique. But Jane—one returns to the problem of Miss Rigby's almost pathological dislike and contempt. None of Becky's *affaires de cœur* (if there were a *cœur*) appeared to shock her; but the love—openly expressed, then sternly abjured, for Rochester appalled her. At the time of writing her article she was within sight, whether she knew it or not, of her own happy marriage. For lack of any evidence to the contrary, and from knowledge of the two parties, we may assume that her romance had developed, was still developing gradually and tranquilly from a congenial friendship. Nothing could be more suitable or decorous. Would it be outrageous to wonder whether her feeling for Lockhart—handsome, reserved, proud, difficult to know, yet to her friendly, sympathetic, admiring—went deeper than she cared to admit, was disturbing in intensity? He was no Rochester; no man lived more cleanly, and none had been more heart-whole in his love of his wife. But some repression in Elizabeth's heart may have welled out in bitterness against the little, plain girl who flamed out in love and knew no repression?

A little over a year later, in March 1850, she returned to the subject in dealing with a further Report of the Institution, and with a volume of Lectures delivered at Queen's College. This foundation complemented the work of the Institution. It was intended primarily for the education of governesses, to raise their status by equipping them with sound knowledge and training them to teach others. Lectures on many subjects were given to 'ladies of twelve years old and upwards' and there were already two hundred and fifty pupils. The fees varied from a guinea to a guinea and a half for a quarter's tuition. Preparatory classes were also arranged for 'young ladies of nine to twelve'. Evening classes were held for governesses. The college was under the care of a Lady Resident and there were Lady Visitors to supervise and chaperon the students, and prevent any scandal with that fearsome creature the male lecturer.

The visiting lecturers were men of sound scholarship, and the classes were very popular. The teaching was just what a girl needed between sixteen and eighteen, when the curriculum of the schoolroom should be expanded, and her studies made more solid. Even more valuable was this new learning after she had left the schoolroom and was not yet absorbed by the grown-up world. At Queen's College she could enjoy the pleasures of study, without drudgery though with good discipline, stimulated by companionship, and by a healthy daily walk (duly chaperoned) to and from classes. Even one lecture, one hour of solid study would give point to her day, and solidity to a life of gaiety.

For governesses enlarging their knowledge and for girls in the late teens it was excellent. Mrs. Eastlake (as Elizabeth had now become) was doubtful of the value of these lectures for younger girls—the nine- or ten-years old, and she was uncertain of the orthodoxy of some of the lecturers—F. D. Maurice and Charles Kingsley among them. From Broad Churchmanship to agnosticism seemed a little step.

The Institution was flourishing; it had a Provident Fund and had already helped some three hundred cases of poverty, was paying thirty-two annuities and sheltered ten old governesses in an Aged Asylum in Kentish Town.

For all her sympathy with this distressed profession Elizabeth did not altogether approve of governesses. With a memory, perhaps of the defects of her own schoolroom, and of the real education she had acquired through copious reading and from her excellent mother, she thought that mothers were the best teachers of their daughters. This opinion was still held, some thirty years later by another distinguished woman of letters, Charlotte Yonge. The question of a mother's competence and knowledge was not discussed; it was assumed that any gentlewoman would be sufficiently learned and accomplished to instruct her daughters and train them in all feminine culture.

Nowadays, however, it was considered a mark of refinement, a social advancement to employ a governess. There was a spread of 'fine ladyism' among the middle classes, which was affected and absurd. Mothers insisted on engaging 'ill-paid governesses for those duties which, one would hope, a peeress only unwillingly relinquishes'.

The peeress might be compelled by the duties of her station to leave her schoolroom under alien rule; for middle-class mammas there was no such excuse. They had leisure without social claims:

'Women from whom society requires nothing but that they should quietly and unremittingly do that for which their station offers them the happy leisure, must now treat themselves to one of those pro-mammas.'

It is one of the most amusing sidelights on Victorian education. Elizabeth must surely have approved, a few years later, the admirable Mrs. Edmonstone in Charlotte Yonge's *Heir of Redclyffe*—the best-seller which Murray rejected.

VIII

PARTIES AND PLEASURES. LONDON
AND THE CONTINENT

HER new life, a full and happy one, was told by Elizabeth Eastlake in letters to her mother and sister: expansive letters, and she used to apologize for any mere scrape of the pen of less than six pages. If they lack the brilliance of her contemporary Mrs. Carlyle's, they are still very good letters. Incidentally, they make no further reference to the Carlyles. Mrs. Eastlake moved in the most exalted society; the Carlyles were occasionally dragged into it by the imperious Lady Ashburton, but were happier in the agreeable borderlands of Bohemia, among fellow-writers and intellectuals. The friendship may not have been broken, but one regrets the absence of mutual reports.

Almost at once the bride was caught into the whirl:

'At present the callers are not overpowering, and we have had quiet evenings,' she wrote, at the beginning of May; 'but these must soon cease.' She made her debut at Lady Davy's, the wealthy and exuberant widow of Sir Humphry Davy, who knew everyone, entertained lavishly, and was regarded with a mixture of amusement and affection by Elizabeth's friend Lockhart. At this party she was introduced to Byron's daughter, Lady Lovelace: 'a plain, odd-looking woman. . . . I looked in vain for the Byron face, though perhaps she has something of the Byron short upper lip'.

Thackeray was also among the guests and was most cordial. A more public debut followed at the Royal Academy Private View: 'the most exclusive meeting of rank and fashion intermingled with artists and their wives'. The rank and fashion, including the Prime Minister Sir Robert Peel, and Lady Peel, were friendly.

'It was rather formidable' but very gratifying. Then a dinner at Lady Davy's assembled a galaxy: Thackeray again—'very diverting', Monckton Milnes—'excessively amusing', Arthur Hallam and 'Eothen' Kinglake who asked if she remembered him, and was told: 'Yes, gradually I have.'

That original autocrat of the breakfast table, Samuel Rogers, called and was gracious:

'He assured me that no event, no great earthquake, no French Revolution, *nothing* could have astonished all Europe more than Eastlake's marriage.' Even if Europe were taking this event calmly, London was sufficiently excited. At a very grand party at Lansdowne House honoured by the Royal Duchesses of Gloucester and of Cambridge, there were whispers of: 'That's Mrs. Eastlake' and 'She was Miss Rigby', which were by no means displeasing.

Royalty she viewed with detachment: The Duchess of Gloucester 'a kind-looking old lady, dressed like one, has left a sweet picture in my mind'; the Duchess of Cambridge was 'a beetle-browed, dark, imperious woman'. Lady Lansdowne herself was fair and aristocratic of look, and 'with her floating gauzes and marabouts seems to walk in a halo of light'. Fashion was still graceful, with flowing lines and soft fabrics of silk, lace and gauze.

Loveliest of all was the Duchess of Sutherland. Crowned with a wreath of diamond mulberries she came floating, swanlike, through the crowded room to speak to the Eastlakes.

'She may be a frivolous and extravagant woman, but she is a most lovely and fascinating one.'

Samuel Rogers invited them to breakfast, an invitation in itself an accolade. Many people angled for it, none refused it. The lovely and witty Lady Dufferin once, to his delight, answered his 'Will you come?' in two words: 'Won't I?' Rogers liked brevity and the body of which it is the soul, and he liked a flourish. Bidden to a musical evening at the Eastlakes at which Elizabeth's friend of Edinburgh days, Mrs. Gartshore, was to sing, he replied:

'To hear that lady I would cross a stormy sea.'

He was at this time in his late eighties, having been born in 1763, but was of undiminished vivacity. Elizabeth wrote of him, long afterwards in *The Quarterly*, recalling his friendliness, his wit, his connoisseurship, his zest for art and for people. By birth he belonged to the English middle class—'that elastic class unique in the world, which when duly qualified morally and intellectually, is sure to have access to all that is best in society'. The entrée to his house was 'a certificate of good society', and sought with unabashed eagerness. 'You don't suppose I seek these fine ladies', he once confided to Elizabeth. 'They seek me.'

There were musical parties, and at Lord Ward's in his private picture gallery, Sims Reeves sang enchantingly. There was oriental grandeur at Lady Lovelace's in the person of the Turkish Ambassador in his national dress, with 'a blaze of diamonds' in front of his fez. He was being lectured by his hostess who would appear to have inherited her mother's reforming zeal:

'"Look at Ada pitching it into him about the rights of women," said Lockhart, and went off with his chuckle.'

Even more exalted and much more intimate was luncheon at Syon House where both the Duchess of Northumberland and the Dowager were most forthcoming; they showed their guests over the house, the remains of the convent from which it took its name and most of the grounds: 'The two nearly did for me.' It was, however, gratifying to be walked off one's legs by two Duchesses.

'We left them at five o'clock, very much delighted with their kindness and condescension, and in great good humour with the English aristocracy.'

At Longman's the publisher, they met Macaulay: 'a happy, honest, sensible-looking man' who harangued the table but could listen as well, and did not resent interruption. Indeed he 'graciously smiled when anyone joined in his theme'.

The Eastlakes gave parties in return, but with some quiet interludes and the beginning of a return to work:

'You will think I am lapsing into bad habits when you see this scrawl of a letter, but in truth my life is less than ever my own, now that I am attempting some industrious habits.' In collaboration with her husband she was translating the German critic Kügler's *Handbook of Italian Art*.

A letter to John Murray thanks him for the gift of a pocket-book which was diary-cum-almanac: 'a most useful companion and will, I doubt not, develop in me certain methodical habits which, I believe, are all that Mr. Eastlake finds wanting in my character'. She was very happy. There is an endearing glow of bridal complacency in one letter:

'My dear husband is at all times craving for my company which he seems to enjoy as if he had not had it the day before, and were not going to have it the day after. I confess I too am in the same predicament.'

At her second Private View in May 1850 she was again with Lady Davy who 'knew all the world', which was interesting. The world included the Duke of Wellington 'whose plump and delicate-tinted face little corresponded with my hatchet notions of him'—the plumpness, no doubt, subduing the famous nose. (Mrs. Carlyle had a similar impression when she met the Duke at Lady Ashburton's ball, and was struck by the gentleness of his face.) Rank and fashion again so thronged the galleries that it was difficult to see the pictures, but Elizabeth did see and admire the Landseer, and Dyce's *Rachel and Jacob*, and the landscapes which she found enchanting.

There is a hint of over-protest at times, almost reminiscent of Mrs. Elton:

'I am afraid we are getting into the whirl, though I struggle hard to keep out of it, or at least to get out of it from time to time. . . . Whilst you are in the sweet country I am toiling at pleasure in this whirlpool of a city. Our engagements multiply about us, and as for my husband's declining any, that's quite out of the question.'

They were shocked by an attack on the Queen—witnessed by John Murray who 'saw the blow given, saw the bonnet flattened to her face, and her face sunk in her lap', and who helped to capture the ruffian; proving that publishers can be men of action in defence of their Queen. The death of Peel, after being thrown from his horse, was another shock and grief. But the season rose brilliantly to its climax. One night, Piccadilly was packed with the carriages for two parties: one at the Lansdownes', one at Miss (later the Baroness) Burdett Coutts'. The Eastlakes were on their way to Devonshire House—'a perfect fairyland of treasures and flowers' with beds of geraniums and pyramids of *camellias bibelots* of every kind on every table, and the owner of all this magnificence, the Duke himself, looking like a Velasquez King of Spain. The dresses, Elizabeth noted, were beautiful but 'so fantastic that they would have passed for fancy dress a few years ago, being worn very much tucked up, with long, flowing ribbons, headdresses with long creepers of flowers interwoven with diamonds hanging as low as the dress behind'.

August was spent peacefully sketching at Deal. That autumn Charles Eastlake was knighted.

'You were the first to give me my new honours, that is, after my dear sister Justina,' the new Lady Eastlake told John Murray. 'You and dear Menie will not grudge coming second to her. I may safely make the declaration that you are both only second to her in my affections.'

Sir Charles was elected President of the Royal Academy, and in the following January the Eastlakes gave two official dinners. At the first were Westmacott, 'a dear old gentleman with a sufficiently good opinion of himself', Maclise and others; at the second, Landseer—full of stories about the Queen—Dyce, Samuel Cooper, and Leslie—this last 'always gentle and timid'. Both dinners were successful, and the exhausted hostess declared:

'Now our dissipation is over, and I reckon on not stretching our dinner-table for at least two months to come.'

W. P. Frith ('Derby Day') recalled these dinners as 'somewhat cold and stately, though occasionally enlivened by the presence of ladies'. At one of them he met Adelaide Proctor, famous for her

'Lost Chord', who was charming in manner although plain in looks; and also the Ruskins, newly married and on friendly formal terms with the Eastlakes.

We are given no details of dress or of dinner-menu. There may have been an enlargement of mind in Lady Eastlake that overlooked such trivialities, or it may have been that the masculine hand of her nephew, who edited her Letters, expunged them. Lacking precise information, we may order dinner with the help of Mrs. Rundell.

The soup might be a white soup from a veal stock cooked with herbs, onions and lemon-peel, strained, then thickened with minced chicken or veal, almond paste, breadcrumbs and cream, with a hint of lemon and mace for savour; or there might be brown soup made from beef (which, after providing the stock would be 'fit for the servants' table'); or, with a memory of Edinburgh dinners, Lady Eastlake might have ordered Scotch Leek Soup, otherwise Cockie-Leekie. Memories of Russia might suggest a sturgeon, roasted on a spit or grilled in slices; turbot was good with lobster sauce and anchovy butter; with an 'r' in the month there could be oysters, perhaps stewed and served in 'rolls sold for the purpose'. A Norfolk turkey would surely appear, as well as roast beef or mutton or a fricandeau of beef or veal. For puddings and sweets there was a delicious abundance of choice: orange or lemon pudding—a paste of the rind mixed with sugar, butter, eggs and grated apple, all baked in a pastry case. Apricot pudding was made with apricots scalded, pounded and mixed with sugar, eggs, breadcrumbs and wine; brandy pudding with layers of French rolls, macaroons and raisins soaked in two glasses of brandy, four eggs and a pint of cream. It was not too late for mince pies, and there were jellies, custards and preserved fruits at choice, with fruit and little cakes.

There was no sherry in the drawing-room before dinner, but with every course, from soup to dessert, marched a lordly procession of wines: sherry, white wine and red, port and madeira. We should like to know whether dinner were still served in the old way of two courses—the second including puddings but not banishing meats—and dessert; or in the new Russian way of serving each course from the sideboard, with vegetables and sauces handed round after the main dish.

As for dress—skirts were expanding, even before the advent of the crinoline, usually flounced, the flounces looped up with ribbon; sometimes there was an over-skirt, but the extreme and ugly elaboration of the sixties and seventies had not yet occurred. Bodices were close-fitting, with a wide *décolletée* at the shoulders, often with a lace collar or *berthe*, sometimes trimmed with ribbons and artificial flowers. Colours and materials were rich; the harsh contrasts beloved by the following two decades or more were not fully in evidence; but brilliant hues were fashionable: crimson, wine-red, purple and green, amber or maize, rich blues, shot-silk.

Silk of every kind was worn: velvet and brocade, satin, and a good deal of lace trimming. Flowers, real or artificial, were added to the corsage or the headdress; jewels, worn sparingly by day, when a brooch, a watch-chain and one or two rings were all a lady would care to display, could be as many and magnificent as their owner's resources allowed: diamond wreaths or ornaments on the head, a parure of garnets or amethysts; with such elegant fripperies as a fan, a vinaigrette in silver or gold, a nosegay in a filagree holder.

The small woman must have been buried under a load of finery, the slim and graceful in danger of being disguised. But at five feet eleven, a woman can carry the richest of silks or velvets in glowing wine-colour or imperial purple, gold or shimmering shot-silk, with brilliant jewels. The mode of the period suited Elizabeth with her stately looks. The hair was dressed low over the ears, then twisted or plaited at the back of the head; the long curls or ringlets of the forties (as worn by Charlotte Brontë's Miss Ingram) were out of fashion except for girls. Ribbons or lace might be worn on the head, or a gold or silver net. When she dined out, Elizabeth might wear a cloak (which could be called a burnouse), a shawl-mantle, or a shawl which, with her height and her eye for drapery, she would carry with an air.

The Eastlakes continued to dine out that winter and spring, even when they no longer stretched their own dining-table with extra leaves. At the de Bunsens' they met Mrs. Norton whom Elizabeth regarded with critical appreciation. Her beauty was beyond question, though 'perhaps of too high an order to strike at first, especially as she is now above forty. It did not give me much artistic pleasure, but I could see that I should probably think her more and more beautiful' with every sight of her. At the moment, she seemed to lack animation; another lady in the company was, in Elizabeth's opinion, more attractive,' though she does not use her eyes so ably and wickedly' as Mrs. Norton.

Turner died in 1852 after a life 'sordid in the extreme and far from respectable'. Shortly before his death he had announced: 'I saw Lady Eastlake.' If it were sight by thought-communication, it cannot have shown her with any look of approval. Turner's will was eccentric, providing for his housekeeper but not for his daughter. The sum of £6 a year was to be paid towards a professorship at the Royal Academy in landscape painting; most of his estate was to provide almshouses for 'decayed oil painters', a class, Lady Eastlake commented, 'who if good for anything can never want almshouses'.

At the opening of Parliament that year the Queen made a deep impression by her dignity of bearing and the clear sweetness of her voice—the two charms that were with her from girlhood to age. 'Her speeches must give the reporters less trouble than any other.' At the Royal Ball she danced a quadrille, her 'upright, beautiful head crowned with diamonds' carried steadily through all the intricacies of the dance. Although she was so small, her figure was 'so delicate and well formed that size is not noticed'. The dance ended, the Queen walked back to her throne on the dais unescorted. It was dramatic but not theatrical; a player queen would have been handed to her throne; Victoria 'went to her place in her own right'—again a quality, that serene, secure majesty, which never deserted her.

Buckingham Palace was splendid 'with marble and gilding ... on all sides, with sheets of mirrors and every nook and alcove full of the loveliest flowers'. Similar pictures are found in other memoirs, notably in those of Lady Frederick Cavendish, of the magnificence of the Victorian Court before it was plunged into the darkness of mourning. The Queen is shown as a brilliant figure, even gay in her enjoyment of stately festivity. It leaves us wondering what might have been the aspect and tradition of that Court had the Prince Consort lived to within sight of old age. Victoria had a spring of gaiety, of high spirits, quenched at its source by grief. With Albert by her side she might have reigned in some degree of splendour, avoiding the contrast between a sombre Palace and a garish Marlborough House.

A State Ball had no rivals, but other parties were not lacking in grandeur: notably a musical evening at Miss Coutts', attended by the Duchess of Cambridge and the Princess Mary (the future Duchess of Teck and mother of Queen Mary), at which the Duke of Wellington went peacefully to sleep and had to be awakened by one of the singers, Lablache.

In the autumn, pleasantly exhausted, the Eastlakes went abroad on the first of their foreign tours together, which were partly in quest of masterpieces for the National Gallery. Elizabeth was a happy traveller, never more so than now, and she fell in love at first sight with that city of enchantment, Venice.

She found it 'a kind of mixture of the old town of Edinburgh and of Cologne' in its 'past grandeur and present filth', while the people 'in their indolence, their dirt and their quickness, would make excellent Irish'.

Nothing could break the spell; nowhere had they found such dirt, deceit and greed, but nowhere such enchantment:

'Venice stands alone—a thing never to be believed in till seen, a dream strangely made up of all the pictures one has known, yet different from all a painter ever did, and which, like a dream, one expects will depart. But be what it may—let its people cheat, its mosquitoes sting, and its canals stink—it is unique in beauty.'

Another important couple were in Venice at this time, John Ruskin and his wife Effie. Elizabeth, disliking Ruskin, enjoyed retailing gossip. Mrs. Ruskin's jewels were stolen, and an English officer in the Austrian army, Captain Foster, was suspected. He was a friend of Ruskin who seemed 'incomprehensibly anxious that no one should think he (Ruskin) suspects him (Foster)'. The police took action. The Austrians, finding it 'a crime in any individual to be robbed by an Austrian officer' tried their comrade by court martial and acquitted him; whereat Ruskin, according to Elizabeth, 'furiously rejoiced'.

Curiouser and curiouser, it was then rumoured that there had been an accomplice in the person of a Venetian lady of easy virtue; also that a box had been sent to Mrs. Ruskin by a Count Thun which might contain the missing jewels.

Sir William Rothenstein in his *Men and Memories* gives a sequel or a revised version of this story: that Ruskin, already repenting a marriage for which he was unfit, was ready to connive at Effie's escape. He knew of the love between her and Millais but would not have the latter involved, for fear of ruining his reputation and career. An Austrian Count was a good substitute; but this particular Count preferred the jewels to the lady.

An almost incredible tale, piquant rather than pretty! The Eastlakes hardly knew what to think, but no doubt enjoyed thinking the worst. Some time later when, at home, they dined with the elder Ruskins, they found them being kind to Effie in the hope that she might 'keep their son from going through some Ruskin labyrinth to Rome'.

There was a profound antagonism between him and the Eastlakes: 'I must keep my hands off Ruskin' Elizabeth had written to John Murray in 1851—and did so for five years, when the victim was caught and rent asunder.

But she liked Effie, and proved a warm, faithful and motherly friend. Two years later, when the young wife was almost distraught by misery and bewilderment it was Lady Eastlake to whom she came for counsel; by her advice, Effie wrote to her parents a full account of the unconsummated marriage, and of one momentous and appalling dialogue with Ruskin. During and after the nullity case which set her free, she found the Eastlakes most valiant champions. Elizabeth defended her against slander and malice; and in turn took up (certainly with gusto) her weapons against Ruskin. She enlisted Lady Davy, Lady Westminster and other influential ladies on Effie's side; was constantly at home to receive and comfort her; wrote her maternal letters:

'My darling Child.

You have my waking and sleeping thought since I last saw you, and the thought that . . . no love, not even that of your admirable parents could take this cup from you, has drawn many a bitter tear from me. But it does comfort me, as I know it comforts your dear mother, that you have been kept in purity and honour, and that no shadow of sin rests on your young brow. . . . God is surely working out some course for you in His love and wisdom, which will enable you hereafter to look back on this troubled time and acknowledge that all did really work together for good to those who love Him . . . Your friends will gather together by a strong sympathy and by the need of mutual comfort. I told my dear husband before I saw your parents' (about the nullity suit) 'and his manly indignation has only added strength to my own feelings.'

She told many others who shared that feeling. In April 1854, she wrote to Effie: 'Much as you were loved and respected, you were never so much so as now—not by me only, but by all whom this sad tale has reached. . . . My dear husband calls you "a heroine of the best kind" and occasionally he *gratifies* me by sentiments of somewhat opposite kind regarding one who I wish could be struck out of your memory as utterly as he will be and already is out of the respect of all good people.'

Among other sympathizers, Mrs. Murray 'hid her face in the

sofa to conceal her sobs—all sympathy and pity'; Mrs. Millman, wife of the Dean, 'was full of tenderness and anxiety'; Lockhart 'expressed himself in curt, grumbling phrases, and hissed out something like "beast"—said there could never be a word said against Effie for whom he was much afflicted, and felt the sincerest interest'.

The Eastlakes refused to receive Ruskin, and one of Effie's supporters wished that all London would follow that example. Effie was free to marry the faithful Millais, but Lady Eastlake counselled a little delay, time for her wounds to heal:

'Another life lies before you, my dearest child—and one that cannot but sparkle brightly to your view . . . but don't think more of it than you can help, be sure that you do more than enough for him in letting him look forward to the privilege of making you really happy—and let neither his happiness nor misery disturb that rest of body and peace of thought which you so much need. . . . Give him just the scantiest *parish* allowance to keep him from starving.' She added that she would like to banish Millais 'with canvas, colours, and brush' to a desert island for two years, then rescue him. This was in August 1854. Effie took her advice at least in part; she was married to Millais in July 1855.

All that, however, takes us away from the immediate activities of the Eastlakes. They left Venice in the late autumn of 1852, and came home to London, to attend, in November, the funeral of the Duke of Wellington. They went, with thousands of others, to St. Paul's at eight o'clock in the morning. The Cathedral was lit by gas 'in one line of diamonds round the Whispering Gallery' but not enough to vanquish the darkness. As the trumpets pealed the Dirge from Mendelssohn's 'St. Paul', the procession entered: Chelsea Pensioners, soldiers, clergy, royalty. The choir sang: 'I am the Resurrection and the Life' and the great Duke went to his rest. It was 'one of those occasions when people speak with one voice in spontaneous obedience to a great impulse alone, and in willing homage to one who can help them no more'.

Next June, 1853, Sir Charles was given an honorary degree by

Oxford, and his wife went proudly to see him 'doctored'. They stayed with the Bishop at Cuddesdon Palace. Oxford was 'a scene of enchantment', still the unspoiled, sweet city of dreaming spires that Matthew Arnold loved, and that young Morris and Burne Jones were even then discovering.

The undergraduates were not dreaming. At the graduation 'the noise exceeded all belief', with about a thousand of them 'having their own way for once,' yelling, cheering, hooting as they pleased. The Chancellor, Lord Derby, looked like a Rembrandt, and when he conferred the degree on his own son Lord Stanley, he addressed him, not with the usual: '*Vir honoratissime*' but as '*Fili mi dilectissime*'—which made a deep impression. The Public Orator, in presenting Sir Charles, referred to his '*coniugem clarissimam*' which somewhat disconcerted the illustrious wife in question, though not disagreeably. Macaulay and Disraeli were among the new doctors, both wildly cheered.

That year, Elizabeth was busy with her translation of *Waagen's Treasures of Art in Great Britain*, that pioneer of art-criticism and valuation—'now grown into a regular cart-horse'. Her letters to Murray are full of complaints about printers' delays.

'The process is to send me three or four proofs at once, after a reminder from me, and then to go to sleep again for ten days or a fortnight.' She insisted on having a large quantity at once 'as I have to refer forwards as well as backwards'. This, in such a work, was reasonable; but there is now the first, a faint hint of an acrimony that was to return and persist for a time. John Murray must 'oblige me by blowing up Messrs. Clowes'. Of that process, if it occurred, there is no record, nor of Messrs. Clowes' opinion of their importunate author.

The crisp touch was never lacking. It is found in a report of a manuscript sent her by Murray, apparently a history in popular form; perhaps an imitation of *Mrs. Markham*:

'I can't say I think much of this attempt to make history amusing. It rather lacks two things, one or other of which are [*sic*] indispensable—*talent* or *pains*. If the party be very young (I fancy I recognize a woman and a Scotchwoman) I am sure they will do a great deal better next time, but if it is an older head and hand, I should fear not much is to be hoped for at any time. The attempt itself may be bold—only very practised hands and cultivated minds can afford to play with great subjects.'

Social life continued with brilliance. The opening of the Crystal Palace in 1854 drew crowds to cheer the Queen; an immense choir led by Clara Novello sang 'God Save the Queen' and the Hallelujah Chorus: 'the *ne plus ultra* of grandeur', formidable indeed to hear with the ear of imagination. An account of the Palace appeared in *The Quarterly* in the following March.

At dinner with the Monckton Milnes the Eastlakes met Charles Kingsley: 'a pale man who stammers'. He was then Rector of Eversley, well known as a leader of the Christian Socialists, a Churchman of liberal views, a vehement Protestant, author of *Yeast, Alton Locke* and *Hypatia*, and was engaged in writing *Westward Ho!* At another dinner Elizabeth met Mrs. Grote, wife of the famous Grecian, herself a notable personality: 'the cleverest woman in England' Elizabeth thought, 'only of masculine, not feminine character'. She could not help feeling flattered by an invitation from Mrs. Grote:

'She eschews all stupid women, and declares she seldom meets with a sensible one.' The new friendship grew in mutual respect, and Elizabeth was to be her friend's biographer.

The Eastlakes went abroad again that autumn, first to Paris of the Second Empire: 'a barbarous sight, the quantity of royal palaces . . . so different from the modesty of the old St. James's and the new Buckingham Palace'. Paris herself retained enchantment, though 'as to French civilization, I can find little in smart furniture and bad smells'.

To John Murray she wrote: 'The only way to secure a throne in France is to build. Louis Philippe built himself up for eighteen years, and to judge from the present man's doings he intends to last longer.' Of 'the present man' seen at the *Comédie Française*, she said: 'The mask he wears is the most impressive I have ever seen.' She appreciated his strategy of building in the new Rue de Rivoli: 'A magnificent undertaking. He mows down houses and anything else that stands in his way, and thus breaks up many a possible stronghold of rebellion.'

They went on through Switzerland into Northern Italy. Elizabeth looked with little favour on the women: 'The girls have that common, uneducated look, mincing and servant-maidish like the Germans'; the older woman were ugly, moustached and impudent. But Venice was as intoxicating as ever: 'One feels like a drunken person here, ready to dance and laugh.' It is a stupendous imagining, her lofty ladyship acting the Bacchante! They met that celebrated Englishman Rawdon Brown who had come to Venice for a few weeks, and stayed fifty years. Mrs. Norton was also there, and again Elizabeth was dispassionately aware of her beauty and brilliance without being charmed:

'She has only talents—genius she has nothing of, or of the genius nature, nothing of the simplicity, the pathos, the rapid changes from mirth to emotion. No, she is a perpetual actress, consummately studying and playing her part, and that always the attempt to fascinate—she cares not whom.'

From Venice they went on to Vicenza, Milan and Chiavanna; thence to Switzerland through the Splüger Pass, first by diligence, then, as the snow grew deeper, by sledge. It was a grim journey and this Englishwoman's courage and calm were praised by the guide; she found it less terrifying than the St. Gothard.

They came home to a pleasure and a grief. Sir Charles was appointed Director of the National Gallery, at the urging of the Prince Consort; and Lockhart died, Elizabeth's oldest and truest friend in the world of letters.

'You may believe I am grieving for one of the most interesting men I have ever known,' she wrote. 'My whole poor literary life is connected with him, and indeed was formed by him; and his ever kind commendation has been the most acceptable feature in a reputation for which I have cared little but for the friends it first

H

helped to draw to me.' Her pen-portrait is one of the most perceptive ever drawn of that brilliant and complex personality, so much loved, so much hated, so little understood:

'No one was more loved by his friends. He had that spell about him which touched the hidden romance in man and woman. . . . I never met anyone who spoke out so courageously for the right whenever it was questioned or cavilled at; and his words were sure to be so trenchant and accurate that there was no appeal from them. He had neither the simplicity nor the folly of a genius, but his instincts were so sound and true that no sophistry or morbid feeling could stand before him.'

For her it was the end of a chapter, or of a song which had sounded very sweetly in her ears. Lockhart had retired two years earlier (in 1852) from his editorship of *The Quarterly*, old beyond his years through illness and grief, and had been succeeded by the Reverend Whitwell Elwin. Lady Eastlake was, and would be to the end of her long life, a valued contributor; but no one could take the place of her old friend.

A new one came into her life about this time, when she met Henry Layard, traveller and archaeologist, author of *Nineveh and Its Remains*. He, too, was of the House of Murray. They met at Dean Millman's—another friend of Lockhart—and talked of the Crimea. Later, the Eastlakes were present at the decoration of Crimean soldiers by the Queen, in St. James's Park: a moving ceremony, the Queen showing great sympathy and gentleness: 'a Queen about whom it is difficult even to be just, for whom no allowance, either in her royal or her female character has to be made; and who has therefore brought into every ceremony of which she is the centre, a beauty of truth, worth and reality, which the world of a century ago or less never would or could have believed compatible with royalty'.

Florence Nightingale's fight for her soldiers against disease and neglect and all manner of deadly things had ended in her own grave illness. Meeting some of her family, the Eastlakes were told of her having been brought to hospital in Therapia by relays of soldiers, men passing her luggage one to the other, in order that each of them might do something for his lady.

Rosa Bonheur visited London that year (1855) and was fêted by the Eastlakes among others. They gave a dinner and reception for her, at which she and Landseer enjoyed a decorous flirtation, Landseer bidding his hostess say that 'he would be too happy to become Sir Edwin Bonheur'. At the French Exhibition, 'the little woman's great picture of the Horse Fair' was viewed with awe; it was fourteen feet long and 'a perfect wonder'. Elizabeth chaperoned her to Landseer's studio which was crammed with studies of 'deer, horses, Highlanders, tops of mountains, etc'—a very fair catalogue—and Rosa wept, not, as we might flippantly suppose in dismay, but in rapture.

That year, too, the Queen and Prince Consort with their two eldest children went to Paris on a state visit to the Emperor and Empress. The streets were packed, and with no traffic control— no calm and capable English police to keep order. Carriages were forbidden to drive down the middle of the road, but of course they did; gendarmes dashed in pursuit yelling protests, mounted police added their imprecations, there was a slanging-match between horse and foot, each blaming the other's negligence, while, in the happy confusion, carriages continued to drive down the forbidden middle way, and the populace ran this way and that as they pleased.

It was a hot night, and ladies sat, in evening dress and jewels, in their open carriages; the scene was like an open-air fête. There was a full moon, but for good measure the city added the illumination of gas, and, on top of the Tour St. Jacques and the roof of the Hôtel de Ville shone an electric globe.

Next morning the Eastlakes stood loyally among the crowd to see their Queen go by. Many of the people climbed upon chairs and were ordered down by the police: '*Et vous aussi, madame, descendez je vous dis*' one of them bade Elizabeth, to the amusement of her neighbours: '*Il veut couper les jambes à Madame*'—with admiring comments on the length of legs that made a chair superfluous for sightseeing. At last the cavalcade passed them with its climax in the 'shining vehicle in which sat the pretty, youthful-looking, best of queens'.

Italy again was at once lovely and disenchanting: 'the land of sapphire skies and opal lakes; of the vine, the fig-tree, the olive and the myrtle; of lies, cheating and deceit; of filthy houses and hideous old women'. They were enraptured by Tuscany, and in Florence fell in love with the Primitives. Sir Charles was making great efforts to procure a Ghirlandaio for the National Gallery. The church that owned it was willing to sell, the Pope gave the necessary permission, but the Accademia of Florence suddenly became rigid about the export of national treasures, and the Eastlakes thought wistfully of smuggling. The pictures, altogether, were a joy; the people not so:

'The young ladies are prudes till they are married, anything you please after that; the young men lead a mere, empty, cigar life'—a nice phrase; cigars were still faintly raffish.

On her return to London Elizabeth wrote a review for *The Quarterly* of Ruskin's *Modern Painters*, which joins her *Jane Eyre* on the rugged and stormy heights of vituperation. She no longer tried to keep her hands off John Ruskin. It was a savage rake of the claws now.

Otherwise she went genially on her way. The Queen visited the Royal Academy in May, before the Private View, bringing with her seven of her children, down to the small Prince Arthur (later Duke of Connaught). It was his sixth birthday and he had been promised a catalogue for himself. When his elder brothers and sisters teased him about it, he jumped on their backs 'which the Queen soon stopped'. She was a firm rather than an indulgent mamma: 'Children, you are always in the way.'

The picture of the year was Noel Paton's *Returning Soldier* which few could regard with dry eyes. Millais, too, was popular.

The Queen's Ball was as splendid as ever. One gentleman criticized severely the designs round the walls of The Twenty Four Hours: female figures on a blue ground. 'It's a great pity,'

agreed Sir Charles, gravely. 'The designs are only Raphael's.'
Among the ambassadors was the negro Envoy from Haiti;
snubbed by the others, he stood his ground, and by seniority of
appointment took precedence over his colleague from America:
'a bitter drop in the Americans' cup'.

That autumn (1856) the Eastlakes went to Scotland, a renewal
of old delights and associations for Elizabeth. In 1857 she contributed to *The Quarterly* an article on Photography which is
admirable as journalism and as a chapter in the history of that new
craft. Work and play continued in a pleasant pattern. In 1858
she wrote a long article on Michelangelo; these articles were in
effect monographs on their respective subjects.

That autumn was spent abroad. From Germany, which she
had not visited for some time, she wrote to John Murray:

'The Germans have not stood still since I was last among
them. They seem to have deteriorated in the art of making coffee,
and still further improved in that of telling lies.' There is a precision, a finality about her insults that compels admiration.

In 1858 the Eastlakes were in Florence where they met Mrs.
Somerville, the mathematician and astronomer, Elizabeth's sole
predecessor as contributor to *The Quarterly*: 'a most gentle, intelligent little lady'. This most charming as well as most learned
of Scotswomen had been born in the late eighteenth century, and
with her memories of childhood and girlhood in Burntisland, in
Edinburgh and in her uncle's manse at Jedburgh, must have had
much in common with Elizabeth who loved Edinburgh, and
had known so many people there who also had been young at the
dawn of the century.

In Florence, Sir Charles bought a Bellini for the National
Gallery. They went on to Rome which failed to enchant Elizabeth. The classical part of the city did fascinate her, and she commented that England was the true descendant of ancient Rome;
but contemporary, papal Rome she disliked extremely: 'nothing
but wretchedness and the worst possible taste'. Even Michelangelo in the Sistine Chapel displeased her. Conditions in the

Campagna were shocking, the roads 'worse than anything
I ever saw in the Highlands'. Altogether, Rome was like 'the
worst view of Scotland' with 'the same squalid dirt, and the same
odious freewill in architecture.' A fine example of double insult,
this comparison of Popish Rome with Calvinist Scotland was
likely to infuriate both sides had they read it.

That winter, only four years after the death of her father,
Lockhart, Charlotte Hope-Scott died at Abbotsford, leaving
three children to continue the line of Sir Walter. Of these three,
her tiny son Walter and a baby daughter followed their mother
within a month or two. Elizabeth wrote sorrowfully and com-
passionately to John Murray of 'poor Hope-Scott's further be-
reavements'; but with a memory of the saying of an old woman
noted long ago, in Edinburgh, she added: 'The first great sorrow
seems to have made so large a breach that these later ones have
passed through it comparatively unheeded.' The small Walter
was said to have been 'the image of dear Lockhart'. And now
'the whole Scott line centres in that fragile little girl'—Mary
Monica Hope-Scott, 'Mamo' whom her grandfather Lockhart
had welcomed and cherished for the first two years of her life.
She was, happily, to grow up and marry, and leave descendants at
Abbotsford.

Elizabeth still deplored, at times, the devouring of her time by
society; her days were too short for all the work she would do:
'their heads and tails cut off by late dinners and later breakfasts''
But the parties were delightful in themselves, and very exalted.
At one, she met the Duke and Duchess of Malakoff and dismissed
them with a rake of the claws. (There are moments when she
reminds us of a large, handsome cat, fed upon cream, purring
luxuriously and amiably—but with claws suddenly unsheathed
from the velvet paws.) 'He looks like a corporal, she looks like
his cook' effectively disposed of the ducal pair.

In 1859 she paid a last, sad visit to her sister in Russia who was
gravely ill; news of her death reached the Eastlakes later, in
Vienna. From thence they went to Italy, to the beloved Venice

and to Milan, where the tri-colour of the new kingdom was flying and portraits of King Victor Emanuel were everywhere displayed: 'a regular Bombastes Furioso'. Then they broke new ground by going to Spain in search of Velasquez whose paintings were a revelation of new beauty. For one of them alone, Sir Charles declared, he would have undertaken the journey.

Velasquez was the only enchantment. The Eastlakes disliked both the country and the people: 'a stern, barren, hungry country torn with storms' and 'a brutal people' who hissed Madame Grisi when she sang in Madrid, but compelled her to stay and fulfil her contract, and who frequented bull-fights. We may recall Miss Rigby's disapproval of Madame Calderon's account of that sport in the travel book she reviewed in the forties.

In 1860 she had a new task: to complete and edit Mrs. Jameson's *History of Our Lord in Art*, which engaged her for a long time. She may have been overworking. The note of acrimony returns to her correspondence, and the rake of the claws caught even the Murrays. The cause of the trouble is not clear, but would seem to have a matter of investments, advised by Mrs. Murray's brothers the Smiths, or connected with their business. When the investments went wrong, Elizabeth not only blamed the brothers but included their sister in her wrath. She must have visited Albemarle Street and made a scene with Menie; and John Murray, finding his wife in tears, very properly took action. He wrote sternly:

'I welcome the assurance of your note that the pain which your "scolding" of yesterday caused Menie was not intended. Let me add to this that it was entirely unmerited, and it distressed us both to think that you, of all persons who have known us so long, should give way to suspicions, and listen to accusations that have no foundation whatever . . . I am not going to lecture you, dear Lady Eastlake. But I implore you by that affection and regard which Menie and I both feel for you, not to risque [*sic*] an interruption of our long maintained friendship by any repetition or return to those fearful colloquies regarding ——'s affairs, a large ingredient in which consists in abusing to Menie her own brothers. These periodical "blowings-up" are as unkind as they are useless. Menie does everything that a kind and thoughtful sister can do to promote her brothers' welfare; but in affairs of business she can have no control, and I for my part interdict her meddling with them.'

The storm blew over; but from time to time, in later years, there was a gust—usually of complaint over the misdemeanours of printers and other vexations in an author's life; and one packet of letters at Albemarle Street is docketed: 'Surly, ill-tempered letters.'

Work did not prevent travel. In 1860 they were in Brussels which they found more attractive than Paris, that 'great, advertising shop all glitter and puff; but behind the scenes all dirt and dilapidation'. Brussels itself might be pleasing, but the table d'hôte produced some unattractive fellow-guests, Russian women 'who ought to cover their faces or cut off their beards'—poor things!

In Paris next summer the Salon was 'an *embarras des horreurs*'. Some of the pictures that were best in execution would have been rejected by the Royal Academy for their subjects, all 'so odious, mere frippery, vicious boudoir scenes, or things of refined cruelty or undisguised indecency'. Home again, Elizabeth went with her husband to the Lord Mayor's Banquet for the Royal Academy and the Royal Society. There being no lady to represent the latter, 'all the honours were heaped on me'; she sat by the Royal guest, the Duke of Cambridge, and stood with him to drink the loving cup:

'He is an immense man so that, as we stood face to face, I could not have chosen a better supporter.'

That year, 1861, ended in mourning for the death of the Prince Consort: a mourning that was to extinguish all the gaiety and splendour Elizabeth had loved in Buckingham Palace. The Queen who had carried her diamond-crowned head in such stately fashion through the dance, became the widow swathed in

crape, crowned with the white caps and streamers of widowhood
that would not be laid aside for any ceremony, but only, as a con-
cession, adorned with a few diamonds; who glowered resentfully
at any suggestion that she appear again in public to give her people
any further glimpse of the splendour of the throne.

Lady Eastlake was in deep sympathy with sorrowing majesty,
and full of admiration for the late Prince. Her tribute to him,
published in *The Quarterly* of January 1862 was much appreciated by the Queen.

After the due period of mourning, social life was resumed. The
Prince of Wales spoke charmingly at the Royal Academy dinner
in 1863. Cardinal Wiseman lectured at the Royal Institution;
it was not a good lecture, being long and diffuse, lasting for two
hours. The artist's eye noted his appearance, 'portly, with a
feeble, sweet voice, and most beautiful hands', and that of his
suite, 'sundry very demure-looking ecclesiastics, among whom,
the palest and thinnest creature imaginable, was our late Archdeacon Manning'. It was many years since he became 'our late
Archdeacon'; he had 'Romanized', to use Lockhart's word, with
Lockhart's son-in-law Hope-Scott in 1851. Wiseman had won a
certain amount of toleration in the twelve or thirteen years following his reckless epistle 'from the Flaminian Gate' on Pius IX's
restoration of the Roman hierarchy in England.

The unification of Italy was a cause popular in England, and
Garibaldi, when he came over in 1864 was fêted as a hero, given
an ovation at the Crystal Palace, and entertained by the Glad-
stones. The Eastlakes were bidden to the party, and her ladyship
regarded the hero with a cool, sardonic eye. He wore his famous
grey cloak lined with red, and 'reminded me of an invalid in a
dressing-gown, with fine ladies ministering to his wants'—ladies
who would have run after General Tom Thumb or any great
criminal had one of these chanced to be the hero of the hour. At
another party she met Benjamin Jowett who pleased her greatly:
'a happy, gentle-looking, grey-haired young man, very agreeable
indeed and very amiable'.

In 1865 she went on her last tour with her husband. At Ouchy they met the young Prince Arthur, now fifteen, walking his gentlemen, Sir Howard Elphinstone and Colonel Seymour, off their feet; and were impressed by the royal manner, boyish and charming, but completely aware of being royal.

At Bologna they found drama in the raw: the trial of a band of brigands including one woman, who looked wickedest of all. The prisoners sat in a huge, iron cage, brought out one by one to stand trial. They were no gang of tattered, evil-faced scoundrels, but all well-dressed, gay, and confident of bearing. Their organization was almost like a charitable club, caring for their members and the dependents of those who might unfortunately be killed in any little affair. Their record of crime was appalling, and they were all likely to be sentenced to long terms of hard labour, if not to death. Meanwhile, they had their hobbies; one gifted youth, an engraver by trade, was said to have modelled a crucifix in bread and a flute in macaroni.

It was the end of the sunlit years. Sir Charles had, for some time been failing in health. The decline became rapid. He fell gravely ill while they were in Italy, and died at Pisa, on Christmas Eve.

IX

LADY EASTLAKE AND *THE QUARTERLY*

MARRIAGE for Elizabeth had meant the best of both worlds; that of the independent woman of letters, secure in her reputation, already a specialist and authority; and that of the wife of a man of high position and private distinction, with the entrée to the inmost sanctuary of society.

In her former capacity she continued to write for *The Quarterly*. Her article in December 1851 must have been the last she sent to Lockhart as editor. It has much of the liveliness of her essay on Dress, some years earlier, and like that, it was recognized and praised by her old friend Dean Ramsay, who wrote to congratulate her, and beg her not to 'let it be the last. Don't let this be so very like angelic visitations'.

She was reviewing some recent books on Physiognomy, and expressing her own views on female beauty.

'It is a woman's business to be beautiful. . . . A woman can hardly be said to call herself a woman who has not, at one time of her life at all events, felt herself to be fair.' To revert to her attack on *Jane Eyre*, may she not have resented the heroine's lack of beauty, her insistence on being plain, 'with features so irregular and so marked', her refusal to dress prettily? To boast of plainness appeared to Elizabeth a perverted pride, almost an indecency.

'Beauty confers an education of its own, and that always a feminine one'. She deplored plainness, but she was sympathetic with girls at the awkward stage. It was cruel to tell a girl that she was plain; cruel if true, and if false, then 'a foolish sham to counteract the supposed demoralizing consciousness of beauty'. It would lose its effect, for the world would soon assure a pretty girl of her looks—to say nothing one might add, of her mirror.

The artist's eye could see the line and structure of beauty underneath a superficial and transitory gawkiness. 'The lanky, dingy, odd-looking girl' might well develop a lasting beauty and distinction, while 'the finished wax doll' would become 'coarse, pudding-faced or withered'.

The girl, however, must do her share, and not lapse or let herself be pushed into 'the kind of young woman who seems to have taken on herself the vows of voluntary ugliness, who neither eats enough to keep her complexion clear, nor smiles enough to set her pleasing muscles in action, who prides herself on a skinny parsimony of attire which she calls neatness, and thinks that alone is respectable which is most unbecoming, is always thin and seldom well' and despises the pretty and the gay. Aunt Elizabeth Eastlake must have been a critical and astringent commentator among her nieces. A girl should be encouraged to be charming, to exercise those 'pleasing muscles', to believe in whatever degree of beauty she possessed and make the most of it. Girlhood was difficult enough without discouragement or self-depreciation. 'There are generally but two stages in life of perfect loveliness and freshness: that of the young child and of the young woman'; but the intermediate stage need not be made worse or neglected.

In maturity, the English type of female beauty was admirable: 'It belongs to women who neither declaim with their voices, protest with their shoulders, nor demonstrate with their hands. It is eminently reserved.' In Mrs. Norton's beauty there was, perhaps, too little of this restraint to satisfy our critic.

The article on *The Crystal Palace* (in March 1855) was in part descriptive, in part a review of a quantity of pamphlets on the various courts—Byzantine, Greek, medieval, Renaissance and the rest—of the Palace, along with sundry guides and handbooks. It might rank as a monograph or thesis, for it reaches more than fifty pages. A contribution to *The Quarterly* was not tossed off in a day or two.

In her eyes the whole scheme was a noble and ennobling one: 'It has been reserved for the promotors of the Crystal Palace, first, boldly to build upon that improvement in society for which Christians have hitherto been resigned more to wish than to hope, and, on this extended scale at least, first directly to attribute to a people the power of being amused without the slightest leaven of vice, cruelty, or false excitement.' This was a compliment to the people, and it came from 'the right hand of the throne', the Prince Consort.

The Palace presented 'just that mixture of nature and art which gives fresh beauty to each. . . . Here lies outspread a garden, free to the humblest feet, such as even the most spendthrift royalty of bygone despotisms never imagined: with every bounty of nature and appliance of art to tempt a multitude to disperse, and with the finest permanent band of music ever organized in England to gather them together'. Admittedly, Sydenham was a long way out of town and the journey cost something, but it was worth the money.

She diverged for a moment to consider popular education: It had been a pedantic period, overloading the young head with instruction; and now we were disposed to welcome 'any scheme acknowledging our more poetic tendencies'. So far, we had tried to unite instruction with amusement, but had failed to cultivate that 'third, beautiful element in which alone their union can be successfully effected'; and now the aim and achievement of the Crystal Palace Exhibition was to develop that element—good taste.

'Whether we be ever intended for a great, creative people in the way of art is a question that does not belong here; but meanwhile, the great old masters are fulfilling their boundless mission to a people they knew not of; and it is not too much to say that Raphael and Titian are ours by right of a far higher worship and more intelligent knowledge than they ever found in their fellow-countrymen.'

To us it may seem to be saying a little too much to assert that mid-Victorian Englishmen were more appreciative of great painting than the Italians of the Renaissance. The complacency, startling enough in itself, is heightened for us by our hind-knowledge that the full tide of Victorian ugliness, in dress and furniture, pictures and architecture was sweeping in.

Some hint of that ugliness Lady Eastlake did perceive and deplore in the polychromatic effects in the galleries of art. Statues, casts and reproductions were painted with a lavishness and crudity that were 'a puzzle to the ignorant and a torture to the enlightened'. 'Red, blue and yellow were ordered by the hogshead' and the result was formidable.

Art was not the only inhabitant of the Palace. There was also the Exhibitors' Department, from Sheffield and Birmingham, and 'the minds that have most revelled in the art-treasures will do themselves little credit if they do not some day find a high and even a kindred pleasure here' among the many inventions, 'the screws and springs, literal as well as metaphorical, of every domestic establishment', for while 'pictures and statues are company that few can keep at their firesides' these were 'the willing, ready, costless servants which throng the commonest homes': needles and keys, carpets and stoves, and, what sounds a capital gadget, a sausage-making machine which chopped and filled at the same time. There was also an enticing toy—'the holiday vagary of some Birmingham heart'—a case of miniature scissors 'the largest of which is fit for the little seamstress of four years old, and the smallest for her doll'.

This article is, on the whole, objective journalism, and she was to return to the descriptive style in more than one future contribution; indeed, her writing on the whole continued to be equable in tone. There was one notable exception, an explosion of personality. Her review of Ruskin's *Modern Painters* in March 1856 ranks among the great prose-hymns of hate. It began with one of those crafty compliments which conceal and convey an insult:

'There are many reasons for the popularity of Mr. Ruskin's works. In the first place, he is a thinker—a character sufficiently rare to obtain, we do not say to deserve for that depends on the issue, that class of thoughtful readers of whom a writer may be justly proud. In the next place, he is a very positive and conscious thinker ... And further, he is a positive and confident thinker on a subject which is now engaging the attention of a large class of the educated English public' namely art. With that increasing love of art went a corresponding sense of ignorance, a desire for guidance. Many readers, especially the earnest young, would 'gratefully follow the guidance of anyone who suggests thought, and lays down principles on a subject which many can feel but few have the power or opportunity to reason'. This was an admirable audience; less praiseworthy was the fashionable one. Art was in vogue.

'Fashion cannot think and must talk, and is therefore the eager adherent of those who save the brains and supply the tongue on the favourite topic of the day.' Furthermore, 'strange and new doctrines ... are always the fashion'; so it was easy to add up the sum of Mr. Ruskin's popularity.

The rake of the claws within the velvet paw was effective. The wound inflicted might not be as deep as a well or as wide as a church door but it would serve to discomfort the enemy.

An artist herself, in some degree, she did not much approve of art-criticism which, unless 'of a most enlightened and therefore rare description, is more depressing than stimulating to the production of art'. Freedom of opinion was wholesome, but 'all that license which abuses the name of liberty' was pernicious: the chatter of the uncreative, the pseudo-artistic gossip in drawing-rooms.

From the carved box of her initial compliment, more and more insults were taken out, lovingly handled, and hurled with precision. Ruskin could, in modern phrase, get away with it because he terrified his opponents by his reputation as a thinker 'of the most able and elaborate class' and his being 'a controversialist of the rudest manners' which any adversary might fear to match. 'Something of the Ruskin is needed to catch a Ruskin.' She recalled Hans Andersen's story of *The Emperor's New Clothes*.

Ruskin was like those crafty tailors: 'He persuades his hearers that it is the test of their religion and morality to see as he sees.' Lady Eastlake cast herself for the part of the child who cried out: 'But he has nothing on.'

The casket of courtesy was now put away; the articles of attack were openly displayed.

'Mr. Ruskin's intellectual powers are of the most brilliant description' (last glimpse of the casket) 'but there is not one single moral quality in their application.' Without that quality there could be no ripening of the mind. This struck hard; for Ruskin in his own opinion and that of his admirers rather shone in the moral line. But no: 'his writings had all the qualities of premature old age—its coldness, callousness and contraction'.

After touching on his 'crotchety contradictions and peevish paradoxes' which proceeded from 'a cold and hardened habit' and 'an unfeeling heart rather than a hasty judgement', Lady Eastlake defined his characteristics as 'active thought, brilliant style, wrong reasoning, false statement and unmannerly language' after which she rightly assumed that it would not 'startle the reader to find us start with the declaration that Mr. Ruskin's principles, as applied to art, are unsound from the outset'.

Among those principles was his belief that painting was the vehicle of thought, valuable only as such; the mere representation of a scene or object being no more like great painting than mere grammatical speech was like poetry. For Lady Eastlake, representation was the essence of painting; it could be extremely varied and original. One idea in, for example, religious art might serve generations of artists; it was common to all, but each presented it in an utterly distinctive way. Allegory in a picture was nearly always boring. Painting had its own language, different from that of poetry, and it was his power over that language that marked the genius. Literary painting, as preached by Ruskin and his followers, said nothing to her; she recalled, approvingly, a saying of her old friend Samuel Rogers, that 'if a picture bore an eloquent description he did not want to see it'.

Ruskin deprecated landscape painting because it had 'never taught us one deep or holy thought' and because 'praise of the artist did not lead to praise of God' (which can be at once denied by those who are compelled by every form of loveliness to glorify Eternal Beauty).

Let Ruskin have his thought to him reserved, was, in effect, her conclusion. Her article is that of a working artist defending the art against the literary amateur who discharges his prejudices, literary, moral, and religious against those painters he happens to dislike. Ruskin condemned Raphael for his acceptance of the claims of the Roman Church—a matter irrelevant to his art.

Proceeding, Elizabeth deprecated the realism advocated by Ruskin and practised by the new pre-Raphaelites whom he admired and who were now achieving fame. In religious art especially, the painter could 'never at once depict what is mean, dirty, and squalid, and yet suggest the grandeur, power, sweetness or grace which are connected with the persons of Holy Writ'. On these qualities we should dwell rather than upon 'all the trivial facts that hung, like dust upon their shoes, to the circumstances of their human condition'. This was a popular point of view, at the time, and expressed itself in the frequent condemnation of Millais' *Christ in the Carpenter's Shop*.

Whatever our opinion of either of the protagonists, we must sympathize with the lady's reaction to Ruskin's decree of infallibility—given in his *Notes on Some of the Pictures Exhibited in The Royal Academy*:

'Hereafter it will be known than when I have thought fit to attack a picture, the worst policy that the friends of the artist can adopt is to defend it.' This, naturally, left her stunned. She does not appear to have guessed the depth and range of Ruskin's insanity.

She ended with a grand crescendo of vituperation: 'Nature has given him the mechanism of thinking in a most peculiar degree. The exercise of this faculty, which is always more or

I

less an exertion and strain to the mind, is none to his; and no wonder, for sophistry travels on roads where, however much dust, there are neither stones nor tolls. . . . It may be doubted whether any mind will have the patience to follow all the windings of one who thinks equally without consistency and without weariness. A man may attack iron bars, oak doors, or stone walls, and hope, with energy and perseverance to break his way through; but to follow a thin thread which leads him through winding and slippery paths, and is always snapping at an honest touch, requires a strength of nerve and tenacity of purpose which Mr. Ruskin's writings will hardly inspire or their refutation reward'. (She had, all the same, made a fairly long pursuit of that thread!)

In conclusion: 'It is the terrible penalty of the propagators of slander that their evil deeds should remain—for no evil, as no good can fall into our mortal world without fruits of which none can compute the length or the strength; in either case . . . is the return or recoil upon the author, and upon Mr. Ruskin the recoil has begun already.'

That, but for some confusion of metaphor, is magnificent, and it is also war.

Her next contribution—to *The Quarterly* of April 1857—was a return to objective journalism. She wrote an account of the 'new and mysterious art' of photography, discussing both daguerrotypes and photographs. It was only fifteen years since 'there were exhibited to our wondering gaze . . . a few heads of elderly gentlemen, executed in a bistre-like colour on paper'. Now photography was 'a household word and a household want, used alike by love, business and justice', found alike 'in the most sumptuous saloon and the dingiest attic'. Photographs of sweethearts were cherished, photographs of suspects and wanted criminals eased the way of detection, reproductions of famous pictures delighted, at small cost, the cultured but non-affluent. (The effects upon journalism were not yet realized; the illustrated paper lay in the future.)

The process was so cheap that a servant girl could now buy for a shilling what 'no money could have commanded for the Rothschild bride of twenty years ago'. It was commonly practised: 'the sun's votaries' were everywhere, in town and village.

As an artist, Lady Eastlake could not wholeheartedly admire the results in representing either people or landscape. The effects were necessarily crude; the marvel lay in their being obtained at all. The whole process still had magic about it. She realized, moreover, the historic value of what could be reproduced so quickly and with such accuracy of detail.

'Every form which is traced by light is the impress of one moment or one hour or one age in the great passage of time.' A photograph of children might not capture their charm, their expression, their character, but it could show their costume, their toys—all that would in time be discarded and lost—with a precision that would be invaluable to the historians of a period. The business of photography was 'to give evidence of facts'.

She could not foresee the development in artistry of the new form, and rightly asserted that it could never take the place of painting. At the moment, miniature and portrait-painters were being deserted for this new mode, but the desertion was only for a time. The public would return, and meanwhile those who remained were more discriminating in their patronage than ever before.

This article is doubly interesting: as material for any history of photography and as proof of the writer's professional instinct, her discipline in journalism, her capacity to absorb a new technique and explain it to the public in a readable way.

The artist in her was critical of the imperfections of photography, and the artist in her held the pen throughout when, a year later, she wrote about Michelangelo, reviewing a Life of him with translations of some of his poems and letters, by John Harford. She repeated her conviction that the artist was not influenced by his creed; he accepted it, worked within it. Personal piety might stimulate genius in religious art, but 'articles of belief have nothing to do with it'. Michelangelo, his predecessors and his contemporaries, 'carried on the forms of Papal tradition, as the Greek sculptors those of their mythology, because they found them ready to their hands'. This review, in its critical and biographical content, amounts to a Life of Michelangelo in its own right.

In July 1858 she wrote briefly (only some twenty-three pages) about the British Museum, giving its history of haphazard growth over the past century, and naming some well-justified criticisms. The Natural History department was deplorable:

'The students may well decline the privilege of pursuing their avocations in the damp, dreary vaults with their interminable, dark and intricate passages. A cell in Newgate is more cheerful, more airy and more commodious.'

Were this section moved to a building of its own, more joy would students, staff and public have, and much less pain.

The Gallery had been in existence only since 1824. It was still a very modest collection; it might have been one of the richest in Europe had the pictures collected by Charles I not been dispersed.

To her succinct history of the Gallery the wife of the Director added some constructive criticism, urging either the enlargement of the building or a removal to the British Museum—which, in turn, should banish the departments of science and natural history, and become 'a grand receptacle for every branch of art' including a national library. The building in Trafalgar Square might become the new Law Courts. Meanwhile, the rooms were mean, the light poor, the walls crowded.

'Let us have one man of character, capacity and knowledge, placed at the head of our art, vested with full authority and responsible to Parliament and the country for the due discharge of the duties confided to him'—and let the trustees know their place. Such a Director had been appointed; it only remained to give him full power.

Her tribute to the Prince Consort, in January 1862, was based on a reading of his newly published speeches:

'There are two classes of character to which the term greatness is applied: the one, possessing gorgeous powers unsustained by any corresponding greatness of the whole man, which crosses our path in this world like a meteor, attracting notice as much by its irregularity as its light; the other, endowed with that perfect balance of mental powers and moral qualities . . . appealing not to our love of the marvellous or thirst for excitement, but to our deeper sympathies and nobler aspirations.' This was the character of the lamented Prince: one 'slow to find favour in a world more quickly caught by dazzling eccentricities than by the steady light of a steady superiority of being'.

Lady Eastlake was aware that a weak-kneed generation might find such moral grandeur overwhelming. She was very severe on 'the Vulgar High . . . a party who have looked on the corruption of princes as their immemorial perquisite'—the gay and raffish section of the aristocracy who had mocked the Prince as a bore and a dowdy intellectual. Even worse were 'the Vulgar Low' who delighted in gossip and calumny and gross caricature, who even believed rumours of his disloyalty, and thronged in 'crowds of credulous and malignant idiots to see the Prince pass on his way to the Tower'.

Sympathetically indignant about the shadow of unpopularity that had lain athwart the royal path, she was ignorant of other shadows: the strong element of jealousy in the Queen's devotion to her husband, the bitter exasperation felt against the Prince of Wales by his far from adoring parents, the frustration of Albert's considerable powers of intellect, his academic interests by the domesticity of the Court.

The tribute rose to a fine peroration of loyalty:

'Alone, the royal widow must bear, in time, to face her loving subjects; alone her loving and most deeply mourning subjects must bear to gaze upon her august person.' It took considerable time for the Queen to endure the sight of her loving subjects in the mass; while their love grew somewhat lukewarm, and most of them bore up remarkably well under their mourning. Before long, the Vulgar Low and the Vulgar High, with many decent people in between, were commenting unfavourably upon the morbid seclusion of her widowhood.

Not so Lady Eastlake: 'We can conceive no higher human spectacle than that of our Sovereign Lady thus bowing her head to the Will of God, and raising it again by the Divine aid.'

Altogether, this is, if we may again resort to Victorian slang, coming it a bit strong. The Sovereign Lady deeply resented any invitation to raise her head and look even tolerably cheerful.

She was, as can easily be understood, deeply touched and pleased by this tribute both to the beloved memory and to her own grief. In the best circles, the article must have been warmly commended. What the Vulgar, low or high, thought of it need not concern us. Neither section was likely to read *The Quarterly Review*.

X

THE SHADOWED YEARS

'YOU have been the good star of my life,' Elizabeth once told John Murray; and on her sad return, in January 1866, she wrote to Menie:

'Whenever you like to come I will see you, and as I have periods of calm, I hope not to disappoint you.'

There was sympathy in abundance from friends, but not all of it spoke to the heart. Out of her grief came a book of reflections: *Fellowship: Letters to My Sister Mourners*, published anonymously by Macmillan in 1868.

'There are those in the world who live for a period in the halcyon and perpetual exercise of devoted tenderness for one lawful and all-engrossing object. Their duty and their love unite in one even, deep stream. . . . To some of these favoured and happy hearts there comes, and always, it seems, suddenly, a change in their whole existence . . . when he who has been the light of their life is gone from them . . . when the pictures look down from the walls, the books from the shelves, when the clocks strike as before, when the same objects are seen through the same window panes, but when your own very identity seems to have departed with him you love, and a miserable, joyless wretch crawls languidly about in your place. And from this bad dream there is no awakening.'

It is acute psychology. Then comes a peculiarly Victorian touch: 'You now feel that you have never sympathized enough with our stricken Queen.'

The picture of grief is vivid; one can almost see the folds of crape, hear the sighing voice. The analysis that follows of the stages of suffering is acute: the initial numbness, obedience to routine, a certain excitement; then the keenest pain; then again the sense of a gulf between the old life and the new, a gulf that separates friends, however kind, from the mourner. The writer went on to offer remedies: the first and essential being prayer, if one *could* pray. Then came the right indulgence of sorrow. Repression was dangerous: 'Let not the cant reproach of "indulging your grief" disturb you . . . If by indulging grief is meant the spending of it, then I say to spend it all you can . . . Grief laid up only bears compound interest. Live in your grief: let the heart ache itself out.'

Work was a solace. The poor often bore sorrow better than the rich, because they must work. 'It is here that we ladies pay for our higher culture, more refined pleasures, and most unwelcome liberty and leisure. . . . Yet work we must, in some shape, in self-defence.' She was already imposing this discipline upon herself.

There was an astringent reference to the well-meaning would-be-comforters glib with religiosity:

'The good people who . . . must be doing what they think their duty by us; and this usually consists in discharging a number of texts at us . . . The Scriptures are a precious medicine chest, our only one, but its contents must be given with discrimination.' If only the well-meaning would 'be content to give that which we can take, or else let them leave us in peace! Precious balms at the wrong season only break the head'. Sorrow could best be borne by being united with the Passion of Christ; the only true comforters were those who knew such a union.

Lady Eastlake assumed, sympathetically, an initial rebellion, but submission must follow: 'God must never be questioned.' In time, one great sorrow made little troubles appear negligible, and in time the sense of compassion was deepened. There must be self-discipline, especially about looking back: 'In that direction lies an enemy worse than any sorrow.'

She ended with an allusion to the Christian hope of re-union: 'This blessed prospect has overlaid every thought, for it is the first and the last . . . in the heart of the bereaved wife.' She could

not, as yet, act as guide upon that path; but 'should these few
pages give my suffering sisters any help on their joyless road, I
may probably venture to ask them to follow me in that mysterious direction'. That plan was not fulfilled.

She took up her social life again, though with much less
splendour and gaiety. At the Deanery in Westminster, where
her old friend Arthur Stanley and his wife Lady Augusta were
hosts, she met the Queen again: 'our thorough-bred lady, who
was all attention to others, and unconsciousness of self'—a
pleasant glimpse, rarely given. This was an intellectual gathering,
with Froude, Tyndall and Lecky among the guests, all pleased
by the royal benignity. 'Nobody, after the Queen was gone,
seemed to want a King again.'

In a spirit of curiosity rather than of forgiveness she attended
one of Ruskin's lectures to an audience chiefly of adoring girls
and young women, who afterwards had the horses taken out of
his carriage and drew their hero home in triumph. Our hardened
generation finds something repulsive about Ruskin and his
'girlies' as he used to call them, and Elizabeth was aware of such
repulsion.

There was a happy visit to the Grotes:

'Her society is a perpetual feast to me.' And in 1871 she began
going abroad again. The Franco-Prussian War was just over,
about which she had written:

'I condemn France but I dislike Germany. I have no fears of
the Germans meddling with us, or even with others for long;
but a great military despotism in the heart of Europe represented
by a people who have never fought for their own national freedom, is a dreadful thing.' How dreadful she could not foresee.
Next year she went to Paris, to a city shattered by the Commune.

In England, there was a luxurious visit to the Meyer de Rothschilds at Mentmore:

'I don't believe the Medicis were so lodged at the height of
their power.' The house was crammed with treasures, her hosts
were the essence of kindness, and she looked with an artist's

admiration upon their daughter Hannah: 'a fine young creature with a kind of Semiramis profile'. This was the future Lady Rosebery.

That autumn she went to Scotland, to Sir John Orde's at Lochgilphead, where she was welcomed by illustrious fellow-guests: the Duke of Argyll, the Archbishop of York, and Motley the historian. A fresh grief came in the death of her valiant old mother, at the age of ninety-five. Mrs. Rigby's memory went back to the England that shuddered at the French Revolution and feared invasion by the Corsican, that cheered for Trafalgar and wept for Nelson. England's later wars were becoming a memory —the Crimea and the Indian Mutiny; but the military tradition was cherished, and a military painting—*The Roll Call* by Miss Elizabeth Thompson was the picture of the year at the Academy of 1874.

All this while she was busy with writing. In 1848 John Murray had published Charles Eastlake's *Contributions to the Literature of the Fine Arts*; in 1870 a new edition was prepared with a memoir by his widow. She had already written a Life of Gibson the sculptor, and was at work upon a revised and enlarged edition of Kügler's *Handbook of Painting: The Italian Schools*, which, some twenty years before, she had helped her husband to translate. Again her correspondence begins to show signs of acrimony; to this period belong most of the 'surly, ill-tempered letters' full of complaints, chiefly about the technicalities of type and title-pages:

'I must beg to remind you that it was your own letter that gave me the assurance that the type was a matter of the printers' taste.' *The Life of Gibson* was to include his own fragment of autobiography, and there was, apparently, some argument about its value:

'I have no wish to induce you to publish Gibson's *Biography* against your better judgement . . . At the same time, the autobiography forms the smaller portion of the book. Indeed I am quite convinced that what he had written would not suit the public taste.'

Still more acrimony was shown about the Kügler. The new edition was much enlarged, in part rewritten, and her ladyship intended to have full credit. A letter, beginning with a chilly 'Dear Sir', objected to Sir Charles's name appearing on the title-page:

'It is plainly impracticable to connect the name of one long passed from this scene, as editor to a work of the present year, and one in which, moreover, not a tenth part remains as in his edition. . . . But the duty and privilege of embodying his labours in this quasi-new book have been thoroughly exercised by myself. . . . It will be obvious to all who care about it that this edition can only have proceeded from me, for no other person could either have been imbued with his teaching, or had possession of his notes. But you have never requested my name as editor. . . . There can be no doubt that my name is, *in every sense*, the right one for this work; and that it also would increase its mercantile value.'

It was a long rake of the claws, and the final scratch at least must have drawn blood:

'But the labour I have bestowed on it, greatly increased and impeded as it has been by your inattention to my letters, has been very arduous, and I do not see that you have any further claims upon me.'

Of John Murray's reply there is no record; nor have we (which would be more piquant) anything of his account of the matter, in private, to Menie.

This attitude to the use of her husband's name sorts oddly with the intense grief and devotion of her *Letters to My Sister Mourners*; but even the dearest departed must not be allowed to filch an undue share of fame.

She may have been suffering from a storm of self-pity, almost a persecution-mania. The next charge against the long-suffering Murrays ('the good star' of her life!) was brought in 1876, in a letter written to Menie from Lake Maggiore:

'If Mr. Murray and yourself were to express regret for the

disrespect shown to my husband's memory, both directly and in my person since my bereavement, it would justify me in renewing intercourse with you, and also go far to relieve my heart of a long-continued weight of grief; but without that regret, I must unreservedly say that it would not be possible for me ever designedly to have the pleasure of seeing you and him again.'

A formidable *coup de grâce*, with a touch of Oriental formality!

John Murray must have spoken of his bewilderment to a friend, for among these letters is one from H. Reeve, referring to Lady Eastlake's 'hallucinations' and to similar delusions about his sisters on the part of her brother, Dr. Rigby, which had made a breach in the family.

In happier mood she went to stay with the Grotes, where she met Jowett again: 'I must confess to a very scandalous liking for "atheists" of this sort'—referring to his reputation for dangerously liberal churchmanship. Whether or not they agreed in such matters, they were both in sympathy with the new, feminist movement for the higher education of women, and their general status. Elizabeth had once deplored the defects of her own schoolroom education, though she was a heartening example of what a woman could do within her circumstances. She had made a career for herself long before her marriage.

But she had been favoured by fortune in many ways; and there should be opportunities for any girl of more than average intelligence and desire for learning. By this time, some of the new schools for girls had been opened—notably that of Miss Buss in north London; Girton was receiving students, Newnham, and two Oxford colleges, Lady Margaret Hall and Somerville, would soon be opened.

As regards the vote, Elizabeth saw no reason against it. 'I have no doubt that women will have the vote before long,' she wrote, a few years later—in 1885: 'I care little about it myself, it is simply a matter of sense and consistency. If women can hold property, then that should give them the vote.' They were likely to use it with fully as much sense as the men, if not with more:

'In the lower classes, a respectable woman is often wiser than a man of the same class. The Board Schools would never be what they are now if woman's common sense were more represented'—which set her off at a tangent about education:

'But I don't approve of Board Schools or compulsory education at all for the poor. . . . I utterly disapprove of gratuitous education for the poor, except that as it is compulsory it ought to be gratuitous as the proper compensation.'

One might mildly inquire what, if anything, she knew about the poor. Her busy life would not appear to have included any of the social work undertaken by so many benevolent ladies of the period; and of country and village life in England she had, since the early days in Norfolk, little or no experience.

That particular letter has taken us, however, out of our decade. In 1878 she made her last voyage to the shores of the Baltic, to visit her nieces. There was a great welcome for her, and not only from her own family. Even the Customs received her with deference, suspending their rules for her benefit without even a whisper of the voice of the rouble.

She was nearly seventy now, still full of intellectual vigour but knowing the recurring sorrow of loss of friends. Mrs. Grote died in 1878, and Elizabeth began a Life of that remarkable woman. Theirs had been a congenial friendship.

Her views on women were once expressed, not without acerbity, in a letter to Henry Layard who had, apparently, accused her of injustice to her own sex:

'Why on earth did you attack me?' she protested. 'I judge of my sister women in a very matter-of-fact way—as to whether, namely, they are good daughters, wives or mothers, and there are few of them who do not fill one of these characters. I have no other test of character. If you fancied me censorious about fast ladies, I beg to say that they are not in my line, and I am still less in theirs.'

Mrs. Grote won full marks. The wife of a famous scholar, herself a strong personality, she contrived to be a devoted wife without any abatement of that personality. She was remarkable not only for her mental gifts but for being 'mistress of herself, the sport of no earthly being; with a perfect consciousness of her own powers and an entire command over them'. For many of her friends, less brilliantly endowed, she was a formidable personage; but—'you feared her till you loved her' which was not long. She was no remote highbrow, repudiating domestic cares:

'Mrs. Grote will know when a hoop is off a pail in her back kitchen', and 'there was always a better way of doing the commonest thing which she could teach'. In this might be included her system of book-lending:

'I'll trouble you for a sovereign,' she would say to the borrower; and the sovereign was kept, safely docketed, until the book was returned.

Mrs. Grote was consistent and of a pattern: 'The good fairies who served her were two-Order and Memory . . . Her mind was always "sorted". She could find what she wanted in that noble organ as surely as in her house.' Her talk, which some people found overwhelming, had all 'the raciness and clearness and even homeliness of the English mind, coupled with the fitness and readiness of the French *esprit*'.

Lady Eastlake has, now and then, a gift for a phrase as revealing as the stroke of a pencil sketch. Her heroine had a particular talent in this way, and the Life preserves some of her sayings: Her 'porcelain woman' is said to have inspired Meredith's 'dainty rogue in porcelain' spoken of Clara Middleton by Mrs. Mountstuart Jenkinson of whom Mrs. Grote may have been the prototype. The lady in fiction said of Sir Willoughby Patterne: 'He has a leg'; the lady in real life spoke of 'a pinchbeck man'. She also described over-submissive wives as being merely 'good adjectives' or 'good doormats' to their husbands.

Elizabeth's brainstorm had blown over. In her correspondence with John Murray about this book there are occasional irritations, but no more than may be expected in any parturient author. The fires however, were still smouldering, and could blaze up in a lively if objective way: as in her comment on Gladstone's visit to Venice:

'How he will talk about Art when he comes home'; and some time later, when Herbert Bismarck was in London:

'I should like to toss Herbert Bismarck and Herbert Gladstone in one blanket, and the two papas in another.' Admirable!

The old vigour was apparent in her account of a pre-Raphaelite Exhibition in 1883:

'The women look as if they were going to be hanged, wringing their hands and poking out their chins; others look as if they had been hanged and were partially decomposed. It is disgraceful to hear so much nonsense talked by people who know nothing of art.'

She was beginning to suffer the pains of an aging body, though her strong frame was to endure for ten years more. In 1883 she went to Aix-les-Bains for treatment for rheumatism, but found no relief. There was the weariness of the flesh; ill, 'and with no chance of dying, which is doubly hard'. The way ahead was too long in prospect. When Browning died in 1889, she wrote wistfully: 'Browning was happy not to have lived to extreme old age. There is extra death in that.'

At least she could be thankful for vitality of mind. Between 1875 and 1889—her own eightieth year—she wrote at least five articles of considerable length and merit.

XI

MANY MATTERS IN *THE QUARTERLY*

AGE hardly diminished her capacity. Her style remained
vigorous, her range of subjects wide; the professional discipline
learned long ago did not fail her, and her articles in *The Quarterly*
dealt with many matters. In October 1875 she discussed 'Drink:
the Vice and the Disease' in a survey of pamphlets and reports on
this problem and on the licensing laws. Both beer and spirits were
cheap; beer and gin shops abounded, and were an easy way of
escape from the misery of the slums.

'A full exchequer and a drunken population are concomitants
that will hardly be found to answer in the end. . . . In the power
of drinking his pocket empty, his health away and his mind
imbecile, the British subject now carries off the palm before his
foreign brethren. Our climate and our cooking have furnished
the excuse, and our convivialities the tradition for deep and
strong potations.'

She claimed, however, that the upper classes were now
moderate drinkers. Public opinion and the new, fashionable
decorum had tamed the four- or five-bottle men of the eighteenth
century and Regency, and it was rare to see a drunk gentleman. (We must incline to think that her view of masculine society
was limited by refinement.) Whatever degree of sobriety
was found among the gentry, it was far otherwise with the
poor:

'We live, as respects the vice of drunkenness, in an age of the
direst iniquity . . . but we live, with few exceptions, in a charmed
circle. Occasionally the news that the cook is lying curiously
asleep upon the kitchen floor, guests perhaps expected to dinner,
startles our serenity by disturbing our comfort' (this was indeed a
frequent tragi-comedy in the Victorian household), 'or the report

of a fearful outrage in which murderer and murdered were alike drunk, raises a passing horror.'

Life for the middle and upper classes was sheltered and decorous but the slightest venture into social work, the quickest glance at the underworld provided matter for discomfort. Children were not kept out of public houses, and boys of twelve and under were frequently drunk. Then the custom of meeting in pubs and inns to hire servants, pay wages, transact the business of Benefit Clubs led to drunkenness all round; the irony of it being that the money that should have been saved in such clubs, for a man's family, was spent on drink.

Lady Eastlake laid part of the blame on these customs; but put the greatest guilt upon 'the sluts of wives' whose habits drove their men out of their miserable homes into the beer shop. Even the good wives were sometimes to blame by being too tolerant of their men's weakness.

It did not appear to occur to her that the poor women might be broken in spirit; that beneath both female sluttishness and masculine drunkenness lay a cause of dire poverty and utter hopelessness. Her belief that public opinion and good example at high levels might reform the drunken poor was singularly optimistic. She was, however, aware of the need for help, and of the work already being done by some valiant women to help men to struggle against this evil: by Miss March among the navvies, Miss Robinson among soldiers, Miss Weston among sailors. And in her circle of security she had somehow heard of the freaks of drunkenness, where the disease became a frenzy, the vice fantastic: the drinking of methylated spirits, of tobacco leaves steeped in whisky, 'and, in the instance of a lady, turpentine and shoe-blacking'.

It was fifteen years since Mrs. Henry Wood had startled the public with the realism of *Danesbury House*, with its lurid descriptions of the gas-lit rowdiness of gin-palaces, the bodily and mental decay of a drunkard, a death in *delirium tremens*. There was by this time a strong movement against drink in any form and any

K

degree; a new puritanism which had its excesses and exaggerations; an attitude of mind which exalted sobriety from an economic and physical prudence into a fundamental virtue.

This article is unusual among Lady Eastlake's contributions, as the only one which discusses social problems. Her next, on Albrecht Dürer, was a return to her own ground. It appeared in October 1879. Like others of its kind, it is a succinct biography. We begin more and more to regret that Elizabeth did not devote herself to this form. She might have written an admirable series of 'Lives of the Artists'. A volume was, indeed, published, of five such articles from *The Quarterly* and from *Fraser's*; but a full-scale Life might have been admirable. Her *Life of Gibson* is, admittedly, dull, but it was written in a mood of strain; and her subject was hardly a genius. She could have portrayed vividly the background of Renaissance Italy, had she chosen to write at length about the Venetian or the Florentine artists.

The Albrecht Dürer article is objective, with only an occasional flash of personal opinion or prejudice: as in her reference to the lack of classical sources and influence in German art, and to the absurdly rigid caste system of the German nobility, keeping themselves aloof from the people, with none of the common feeling that was found among the English aristocracy. She continued to dislike the Germans and made no effort at impartiality or concealment.

In 1882 she reviewed Taine's *Ancien Régime* and *History of the French Revolution*, with other accounts of the Terror. This article, entitled 'The Jacobin Conquest' is an admirable historical essay. She had the makings of an historian—though not an impartial one—and particularly a social historian; people interested her, and the conditions of life. She had a sense of the past, an insight into cause and effect. Comparing the French Revolution with the Polish rising against Russian tyranny, she made the point that the former succeeded because it was the revolt of a nation against despotism, while the latter failed, being the movement only of a caste, the nobles, against a foreign enemy.

The Terror was a hundred years away, far enough to be seen in perspective, and she could see the evil on both sides:

'The despotism which prevailed in France outraged the very laws of nature in its system; it made it the interest of the higher born brother to oppress, and the instinct of the lower born to detest. . . . We know now what the demon and the wild beast latent in man can bring us to.'

Of Louis XVI she wrote wisely:

'His character so far made the Revolution possible as it was the one least qualified to arrest, divert or direct its course. . . . Nature had given him much that is desirable in a constitutional monarch, but little of that which is requisite in a despot. . . . He had but scanty light to guide him in the dark and lurid atmosphere that environed him, but dim as that was, it was "light from Heaven" and he walked humbly, often stupidly by it!' Of Marie Antoinette she gave one pathetic glimpse. A small boy, held in his mother's arms to see her pass to execution, bowed and kissed his hand to his Queen; the pale face that had shown no quiver of fear, flushed at the tiny homage.

There was one extremely Rigbyish comparison which recalls the Elizabeth who stalked into Presbyterian kirks to criticize and remained to condemn:

'In the same way that the Scotch Presbyterian Church was modelled on the principle of opposition to Rome, so the new French Constitution was framed in opposition to the *Ancien Régime*.'

She was on her home ground again in 1886, with an article on the National Gallery, discussing a new Report and Catalogue and referring to her own earlier article in 1859.

There were still defects, but the collection of pictures had vastly increased. In 1859 it had contained 593 pictures; now there were over 1,200, more than half of them Old Masters. Of these, the most notable were *The Virgin of the Rocks* by Leonardo da Vinci, and the *Madonna degli Ansidei* of Raphael, usually known as 'The Blenheim Madonna', having been bought from the Blenheim

Palace collection. This, and the Van Dyck equestrian portrait of Charles I had been bought together for £87,500, and the annual Treasury grant to the Gallery had been suspended until this should be paid; which 'we cannot but think . . . was an unfair, unwise, parsimonious act on the part of Mr. Gladstone's Government'.

The Flemish, Dutch and German schools were still poorly represented—Dürer being a notable lack—and there was little Spanish painting. The Director might profitably visit Madrid and Seville; she must have recalled that holiday in Spain with her husband when they discovered Velasquez. The English painters, too, ought to be more fully represented, especially in portraiture and landscape; she praised the Norfolk school of painting, especially Crome and Cotman.

As regards the 'exhibition, preservation and safe custody' of the national collection, there was much to deplore. She still found Trafalgar Square an unsuitable site:

'Unfortunately, complete ignorance of what a National Gallery ought to be, and of what, in a highly civilized and wealthy country like England it must eventually become . . . seems to have existed on the part of those who undertook to erect, and of the architect who designed the edifice to contain it.'

In recent years, new rooms had been added, and half of the building had been left free by the removal of the Royal Academy to Burlington House; but the Gallery was still inadequate, and too much of a patchwork. It must be enlarged, or better, transferred to a new building.

As for the administration, she was able to pay a tribute, veiled in anonymity, to her husband:

'No more accomplished gentleman and scholar, no one better acquainted with the history and literature of art, no more enlightened and discerning connoisseur could have been found for the office. To him the national collection owes the high position among the public Galleries of Europe which it now holds.'

Sir Charles had been succeeded by Sir William Boxall who died after a brief term of office, then by Sir Frederick Burton, through whose influence the Blenheim masterpieces had been bought for the nation.

The Gallery was much more public than in its early years, being open every day except Sunday, and free except on Thursday and Friday which were copying days for students, and when the public were charged sixpence. Students flocked to copy the paintings, more indeed than could easily be accommodated, which was another reason for building a new and larger Gallery.

It was interesting to discover the relative popularity of certain pictures:

'We regret' (why?) 'to say that during last year, the one most frequently copied was Greuze's *Girl With an Apple*.' Van Dyck and Rembrandt were almost equally popular; among English painters, Landseer came easily first, with his *Spaniels* and *Dignity and Impudence*. One can easily believe that these copies sold well. Home was incompletely furnished without at least one copy or print of some of Sir Edwin's dear doggies, so amusing or so touching, and the Queen loved them too. Reynolds' *Age of Innocence* was also a favourite; but Gainsborough came low on the list.

Finally, Lady Eastlake regretted the loss to the Gallery and acquisition by the Rothschilds of Rubens' portraits of his family and himself, and of Helen Fourmant. Again Gladstone was to blame:

'We believe that Lord Beaconsfield, with that wise liberality that distinguished him, would not have hesitated to acquire these two pictures for the nation.'

To review one's own book might nowadays be regarded as a breach of propriety, and of that honour which prevails even among reviewers; but when the review is a *précis* rather than a criticism, it may perhaps be condoned. Anyhow, Lady Eastlake and, presumably, John Murray saw nothing amiss in her dealing with her own English edition of Alois Brandl's *S. T. Coleridge and the English Romantic School*, along with Lives of the poet by H. D. Traill and by Hall Caine.

She wrote with warmth and humour, quoting some pleasant details. Who but Coleridge, she asked, 'a poor student at Cambridge, would have given a house decorator *carte blanche* to do up his rooms, and then have accepted a recruit's bounty money ostensibly to pay his debt, which it never did or could have done, but really because he had a prejudice against soldiers and horses which he felt it right to overcome'? And who else 'would have volunteered a public sermon to the Glory of God, and then have used the pulpit to launch a philippic against the tax on hair-powder; or have announced a lecture on "Romeo and Juliet" and entered instead upon a defence of flogging at school, and an essay upon the European languages'?

She concluded with a tribute to Coleridge that is altogether Victorian in flavour:

'Coleridge's faults, open as the day, were negative, however grave. He erred by what he left undone, rather than what he did. . . . He was pure in thought, word and deed. Not a word did he ever write or say that the most modest woman might not hear or read.'

In this number of *The Quarterly* there appeared also, following the *Coleridge*, a review of a new edition, the fifth, of Kügler's *Handbook of Painting*, 'thoroughly revised and partly rewritten' by Sir Henry Layard. In this, courteous reference was made to the original edition by Sir Charles, and the first revised one by Lady Eastlake.

A good journalist must have many capacities and at least the rudiments of more than one style and *genre* of writing. Elizabeth, as we have seen, had no mean sense of history. She had also talent, if a modest one, for story-telling. In her early writing days, after the success of *Letters From the Shores of the Baltic*, she had published, anonymously, a volume of *Livonian Tales*, and a single story, *The Jewess*, all derived from her experiences. In 1888 she wrote for *The Quarterly* an account of a strange character, one almost too fantastic for fiction, Kaspar Hausser, about whom six monographs had been published in Germany. This enigma had suddenly appeared, sixty years ago, in Nüremberg, bearing a letter to the Captain of the Light Horse which said he wished to become a soldier like his father. He was almost dumb, uttering only a few sounds. Being offered food, he declined meat, beer and wine, and accepted only bread and water. He looked about seventeen, showed little intelligence, but when pleased, wore a sweet expression. He could write in a childish hand, and his ways were childish. When shown his reflection in a mirror, he looked behind it to find who this person regarding him might be; he burned his hand, touching a flame, as a baby would. His eyes appeared weak in daylight, but he saw clearly in the dark, and his hearing was acute.

For a time he drifted about the town, then disappeared; to reappear, wounded. His story was that a man had appeared to him on the mountain, given him a purse containing a message, then stabbed him. The poor creature died of his wounds; and nothing could be made of his story or of the message.

Had she lived for another decade, even for five years more, Elizabeth might have had the pleasure of reading and reviewing some detective fiction. Her comments on Sherlock Holmes would have been delightful.

In the following January (1889) she wrote, *con amore,* about her adored queen-city, Venice. She was reviewing some books: two by Italian scholars, based on civic documents; one by Mrs. Oliphant—who had so much of her own versatility, *The Makers of Venice*; and two by Horatio Brown, *Life on the Lagoons,* and *Venetian Studies*.

It was an excellent *résumé* of Venetian history. She had absorbed all the matter of the books under her notice, and then mixed with that her own memories and knowledge:

'The annals of Venice are human history with all the softer parts left out. A peculiar feature, which may be fairly accepted as solving part of this problem, at once meets us in the total absence of all female influence, whether domestic or political.'

The influence of the East was strong and had caused something like the oriental seclusion of women.

There was a good deal of the feminist in the old lady, as there had been in the young one who criticized German women for their social apathy. On its own merits, this article ranks high; as the work of a lady of eighty, it is more than a little remarkable.

XII

THE LAST YEARS

I

THE CONTEMPORARY SCENE. OTHER JOURNALISTS

IN the last three years of her life, at the beginning of the last decade of the century, Lady Eastlake was to write five articles: two in *The Quarterly,* two in *Longman's Magazine,* one in *Murray's Magazine,* a new periodical from Albemarle Street which had a brief though charming life. Since 1842, when she first contributed to *The Quarterly,* she had not ceased to be a journalist. In that half century, the profession had greatly developed, and offered an entrance to many women.

In the forties, there had been fashion magazines, and also keepsake-albums in which feminine talent of a kind might display itself, especially in verse; there had been the solid Reviews— *The Quarterly, The Edinburgh, Fraser's*—of strong political colour and considerable intellectual weight. Between these extremes there was a vacancy; this was filled, within the next decade, with new periodicals with no exclusive devotion to either fashion or literature, which dealt chiefly with topics of the day in a style more colloquial than that of the older Reviews, with less formidable weight, and with rather more direct impact. In this new journalism women began to play their part, efficiently and zestfully, as they became more and more aware of the world outside their homes, more and more eager to take part in the affairs of that world.

One of the most eminent was Frances Power Cobbe, Elizabeth's junior by thirteen years, the daughter of an Irish family of the ascendency. After a semi-education at a Miss Pinkerton's Academy in Brighton, she came home to educate herself profoundly, by reading and private study, and also to become a most efficient housewife. During this domestic period she wrote her first book: *Essay on the Theory of Intuitive Morals.* Her father's death uprooted her. For a time she travelled abroad, then went to Bristol for a period of social work, part of it with Mary Carpenter in her Reformatory Schools, part of it in workhouses and hospitals. Intellectually a philosopher, morally a reformer, she wrote always with a purpose, and in 1861 contributed 'Workhouse Sketches' to *Macmillan's Magazine.* This was the beginning of a career in journalism of the new kind, different from that of Elizabeth. It continued with some travel sketches, and a flow of articles on 'women's affairs and claims' (to use her own phrase), and on social, economic, philosophical and religious problems.

During the 1860's and 1870's she lived in London, an independent woman engrossed in her profession, earning enough, with the addition of her patrimony, to indulge her love of travel and to keep a personal maid—who added not only comfort but convention to her way of life. This life in some ways resembled that of Elizabeth in Edinburgh, twenty years earlier, with a similar social and professional security but with wider interests and with that passion for reform which was to possess so many of her contemporaries.

Frances Cobbe contributed to *The Quarterly, The Contemporary Review, Fraser's, Macmillan's, The Fortnightly, The Cornhill, The New Quarterly Magazine, The Theological Review, The Modern Review,* the *Spectator,* and the *Daily News*: a formidable list and her articles were by no means airy trifles. She found life intensely exhilarating:

'To be in touch with the most striking events of the whole world, and enjoy the privilege of giving your opinion of them to 50,000 or 100,000 readers within a few hours, this struck me . . . as something for which many prophets and preachers of old would have given a house full of silver and gold.' And she was paid for it. This opportunity came to her through the daily press. She was, first, correspondent to the *Daily News,* then, in 1868 joined the staff of the newly founded *Echo*, the first halfpenny newspaper. On three mornings a week she went to the office in the Strand, and there, in her own room wrote a leader on some question of the day; not, however, on politics. This job lasted for seven years during which she wrote more than a thousand leaders: for preference, on ethics or on some matter which offered 'an opening for a little fun'—for beneath her solid exterior there lurked still 'the bould Puckawn' that her nursery-maid had found her in her Irish childhood.

The creative spirit did not touch her which is to be regretted, for, with a touch of genius quickening her talent, she might have written delightful and hilarious tales of Irish country life; but 'I have been from first to last an essayist,' she wrote in her auto-biography. 'I have done very little in any other way than try to put forward . . . an appeal for some object, an argument for some truth, a vindication of some principle.'

Book-reviewing she disliked, 'partly for the rather sordid reason that it involves the double labour of reading and writing for the same pay', partly because she felt herself lacking in the critical spirit. Moreover, 'the pain and deadly injury I have seen inflicted by a severe review is a form of cruelty for which I have no predelection. It is necessary, no doubt, in the literary com-munity that there should be warders and executioners at the public command, to birch juvenile offenders and flog garrotters and hang anarchists; but I never felt any vocation for these dis-agreeable jobs'—unlike Elizabeth who, on at least two occasions, played the executioner with zeal and zest.

In temperament, outlook and activity Miss Cobbe hardly resembles Miss Rigby or Lady Eastlake. She was closer to Harriet Martineau for whom in middle life, the new journalism offered the scope she desired. By the 1850's, Miss Martineau had a long record of writing stories, pamphlets, volumes of useful know-ledge, a novel, books of travel. She was one of the best-known women of the period; much admired and much disliked according to the on-looker's religious and political opinions, being herself a radical and a Unitarian. Now, she began a regular series of articles, from three to six a week for the *Daily News*, continuing in this until the 1860's. She and Lady Eastlake were utterly divergent in outlook, beliefs and principles; her ladyship probably thought Miss Martineau devoid of principles. They were, for all that, of the same temper and quality: alike in their strength of intellect, their force of character, their vitality.

Journalism was becoming more and more a possible profession for women but literature had always offered a way of escape to those who might otherwise have been imprisoned by circumstances. That other notable lady of Albemarle Street, Mrs. Norton had written what might be called journalistic verse in her *Voice From the Factories* and *The Child of the Islands*. She also wrote many pamphlets on the right of women to the custody of their children, in case of a broken marriage, and to control of their own property. She and Miss Martineau are more closely linked with the new generation of women journalists than is Lady Eastlake in her more secluded region. The new generation were writing with an immediate purpose for which they needed a swift vehicle.

Such a vehicle was found in *The Englishwoman's Journal,* founded in 1857 by Bessie Rayner Parkes, (afterwards Madame Belloc and mother of Mrs. Belloc Lowndes and of Hilaire Belloc), and Barbara Leigh Smith (Madame Bodichon) with a few sympathetic colleagues. These two friends were, respectively, twenty and eighteen years younger than Lady Eastlake. Their *Journal* became the organ of the Women's Movement for reform and advance in everything affecting women and girls. It published articles and reports of topical and feminine or feminist interest: on 'The Condition of Working Women in England and France'; on 'The National Association for the Promotion of Social Science'; on 'The Society for Promoting the Employment of Women'. It discussed with sympathy the only two genteel occupations then open to girls and women—those of the dressmaker and the governess. As it advanced in years it expanded in scope, and included biographical sketches of such famous women as Florence Nightingale, Elizabeth Blackwell, Rosa Bonheur, Rachel. It reflected the increasing amount of social work done by women, in hospitals, asylums, penitentiaries, and the advance into professional dignity of teaching and nursing. With the opening of high schools and colleges for girls, the former was a career for the well-educated, with a special training added to their book-learning, while nursing had been lifted by Florence Nightingale and her ladies far above the mire in which Sairey Gamp and Betsy Prig had waddled.

Altogether, *The Englishwoman's Journal* might have received the praise later bestowed by Queen Victoria upon Princess May: 'very unfrivolous'. It was not, for all that, grim, nor did it despise general and genial subjects. Reviews were generally of books with a purpose, but poetry was admitted—not, it must be said, of the rarest quality. Barbara Bodichon wrote a charming sketch of *Life in Brittany*. There were travel articles, historical vignettes of *The Manner of Life of Englishwomen* in successive periods of history and some notices of French books. Frivolity might not break in, but there was some cheerfulness with a marked lack of bitterness and frustration, and with a general atmosphere of culture. None of the contributions was lengthy; neither readers nor writers had time for a massive prolixity.

The Contemporary Review, founded in 1866, was distinctly high-brow, with a leaning towards philosophy and theology of the liberal kind, and by 1890, the year we have reached, it included the work of such brilliant women of the new generation, as Vernon Lee and Millicent Fawcett, as well as the indomitable and indefatigable Miss Cobbe, who was then discussing 'The Two Religions. . . . Namely the Worship of Power and the Worship of Goodness'. That year Vernon Lee wrote a short serial: *A Worldly Woman*.

Only a select type of women could appreciate such periodicals; for the masses (including, no doubt, some of the select as well) Samuel Beeton, husband of the most famous of culinary authors, began *The Englishwoman's Domestic Magazine*, with the aid of his immortal wife. It was an excellent package of material domestic, practical, sensible, with a touch of frivolity for trimming, and a hint of intellectual interests to be worn lightly like a flower. The first number contained a biographical sketch of Maria Edgeworth, a story: 'The Mystery of the Gowns', some cheerful advice on 'How to Manage a Husband', many recipes and hints on the toilette, the care of household pets, on gardening and the cultivation of plants. There were fashion prints and dressmaking diagrams, and a correspondence column headed coyly, 'Cupid's Letter Bag', of a type which still flourishes. It was all very cosy, sometimes a little arch but never silly, and always excellent of its kind. Its influence is incalculable, and its descendants are innumerable.

The Queen, founded in 1861, was on the same lines on a slightly higher social level—which rose with the years—and rather more varied contents: articles on Society with a capital, on Royalty, on the theatre and opera as well as on domestic matters. By 1890 *The Queen* was extremely upper class, with much news of the Court and of foreign as well as domestic royalty. One has, indeed, only to glance at such magazines to realize how numerous were the royal personages, major and minor, of Europe, and how intricately they were related by kinship or marriage. *The Queen's* travel-notes dealt chiefly with the South of France, Egypt, and other resorts of the fashionable; recipes were luscious and elaborate, for dinner parties, not for homely, everyday meals; fashions were of the utmost elegance and latest vogue, assuming a certain degree of wealth in readers of *The Queen*. But it was not all frivolity; a series of reports on Women's Employment showed how greatly this had expanded: women might now train as secretaries, as chemists, and as highly professional, specialized teachers and nurses. Women were coming into city offices as typists; the typewriter had proved an instrument of emancipation, a means of breadwinning. It was more than a machine; it was, if one may be briefly whimsical, a key to open doors, a walking-stick to give support on a long march; and its influence on feminine life was no less marked than that of the sewing-machine which made dressmaking so much easier, and the copying of models so much more practicable.

Somewhat apart from this new journalism, and even farther apart from the old, massive sort to which Lady Eastlake adhered, was the magazine for the schoolroom, for the girl on the threshold of the world, which was created by Charlotte Yonge in her *Monthly Packet*. This had perhaps done its work in continuing a gentle education, that was far from being either narrow or superficial, beyond the days of lessons with the governess; in the new world of high school and colleges it came to a dignified end, leaving a fragrant memory. To this unique achievement, to the considerable and delightful volume of literature *jeune fille*—as distinct from books for children—Lady Eastlake made no contribution; which one regrets, for her criticisms and appreciations of children's books, long ago, had shown in her a lively sympathy with the juvenile mind.

With the new journalism she had probably much sympathy, though she took no active part in it. She had always thought well of the intelligence and common sense of her own sex, in its best members, she saw no reason why women of property should not have the vote, and she would have welcomed, in her own girl-hood, the regular education now available to girls.

But almost inevitably she begins, now, to stand aside and in the background. The atmosphere of the literary world was changing, and with it the form in which she had made her name. *The Quarterly* still published the long, authoritative and scholarly article or study, but other periodicals preferred a briefer form: a *causerie* by a writer of cultivated mind and wide, general knowledge, with a gift for allusion rather than exposition. The 1890's and early 1900's were the decades of the essay; it was the *genre* of the period, as the novel had been of earlier decades, and it flowered most profusely and exquisitely in that ground. There was a return to the urbanity, the wit, the grace of the eighteenth century and the Regency; the true heirs of Steele and Addison, Lamb and Hazlitte were now discovered, and many of them were women. One, indeed, was a genius: Alice Meynell whose first volume of essays was published in the year Elizabeth Eastlake died.

Yet our valiant old lady stands only a little aside, withdraws into the background but not altogether from the scene. Her work continued to the end of her life, showing the old vitality, the unrelaxed discipline, with the hint of a mellowness which might, had she been ten years younger, have ripened into a new urbanity.

II

LAST PAGES

Her last but one contribution to *The Quarterly* was a return to her first subject: Russia. Again she discussed a group of books on the Russian scene: *L'Empire des Tsars et les Russes* by Anatole Leroy-Beaulieu; an *Open Letter to the Head of the Russian Church* by Hermann Dalton; two of Turgenev's novels in a French translation—*Terres Vierges* and *Pères et Enfants*; and, also in French, the Journal of Marie Bashkirtseff.

There was a reserve of knowledge and of memory behind her writing; she knew her subject with a personal intimacy, and wrote with a certain warmth even when she disapproved of this aspect or that:

'Russia has no youthful past. She has known no Crusades, no reign of Chivalry; and grand and generous traditions are as much wanting to her history as the Gulf Stream is to her climate.'

No visitor, in her remembrance, was ever asked his opinion of Russia; it was impossible to start a discussion of Russian affairs in Russian company. She found in Nihilism a clear exemplification of the contrasts she had noted in Russian life 'a mixture of the positive and practical with the absurdest theories—a union of noble elements of humanity with some of its falsest forms'.

Nihilists were most of them young, many of them girls, and to
their youthful idealism was 'doubtless owing that comparative
purity of morals observable among them'.

Turgenev she found charming, greatly preferring him to
Tolstoi 'both as regards genial humour and purity of moral
taste', and she appreciated in his heroines that enchanting freshness and grace which make his novels delightful.

These virtues were not apparent in the heroine and writer of
the famous Journal. Already Lady Eastlake had commented
privately on Marie Bashkirtseff: 'a vain, frivolous, forward
young lady, fancying herself in love with the Duke of Hamilton
when she was twelve years old . . . the most detestable, unhealthy rubbish I ever read—very like what I have always known
of Russian girls in the schoolroom. Some fashionable ladies have
gone wild over it as an interesting "psychological narration".
Psychological fiddlestick' concluded her ladyship with asperity.

Long ago she had deplored the lack of nursery life in the
Lithuanian homes she had visited, and the forcing of children into
adult dress, habits and attitudes. Now she found in 'the utterly
false education of Russian children of the higher class' the source
and explanation of Marie's exhibitionism.

'The unfortunate little beings see and hear all that goes on
among the most frivolous and vicious society in Europe', and
were corrupted; Marie, more than her contemporaries, by the
very writing of her Journal and the sensation she caused:

'Poor spoilt child . . . It seems hard not to grant her any of the
admiration she so ardently coveted. Nor is there any doubt that
the energy and self-confidence which enabled so young a creature
to commence and carry through a work of this extent—for it
covers 992 mortally weary pages—might, rightly directed, have
gained her legitimate fame; as it is, she has left a monument of
egotism and vanity and worse, for which we know no parallel.'

Marie Bashkirtseff might have come from the voluminous
pages of Mrs. Sherwood—*mutatis*, of course, *mutandis*, including
the matter of the Duke of Hamilton!

L

Lady Eastlake's last contribution to *The Quarterly*, in July of the same year, 1891, began as a review of recent German and Italian art-criticism, and ended as a tribute to an old friend, the scholar and connoisseur Giovanni Morelli, the Bernard Berenson of those days. She gave a brief biography, with a summary of his pronouncements, an estimate of his achievement:

'True connoisseurship or the identification of a master may be indirectly a matter of intuition, tradition and documentary evidence; but is directly dependent on a mode of research infinitely more intellectual, exact, and not altogether independent of common sense and conscientiousness.'

In the same issue appeared a brief notice of Samuel Smiles' Life of John Murray the Second and of his father: *A Publisher and His Friends*. Elizabeth, the old friend of three generations now, wrote to John the Fourth of her pleasure in those memoirs.

'Few or none who have lived until now can have a more vivid recollection of his kindness and liberality. I grudge approaching the end of these volumes, for they have been delightful companions . . . Dear Lockhart appears to great advantage in these pages.'

Gladstone, reviewing the book in *Murray's Magazine*, said he himself must be the last man now living to have been published by John the Second—the Emperor or Anak, but that two distinguished ladies could make that claim: Mrs. Butler (Fanny Kemble) and Lady Eastlake.

In September 1891 Elizabeth herself wrote for *Murray's Magazine* an article on 'Temper'. (Did Menie read it with wry amusement, and tell her son of a certain interview with the author long ago, and of his father's stern rebuke?) Elizabeth opened with the statement that there was no precise word for 'temper' in any other language. The French *mauvais humeur* meant a flash of passion, for the Frenchman was too sociable an animal to be sulky, moody or disagreeable. The German knew many degrees of irascibility, and could brood over grievances, but had no exact word for it. Only the English named it, and in England it meant an unsociable vice which could flourish only in an unsociable English home.

'Most justly and logically may [temper] be defined as the greatest curse of the English race which destroys the domestic happiness which is its greatest blessing ... Temper may be said to be always selfish, always ill-bred, often cruel, sometimes brutal; the indulgence of one, and the misery of many, the freedom of one, and the bondage of many.' It was a picture, sufficiently true and depressing, of many a home ruled by paternal tyranny, in which 'perfect fear casts out love'.

An invitation to write for *Blackwood's Magazine*—the 'Maga' of Lockhart and Wilson—was declined:

'I do not fancy their double columns,' she told John the Fourth. 'And there is no Blackwood left who remembers me.'

Edinburgh, had she revisited it, would have been a city of ghosts and memories; the spruce and lively 'little Lord' Jeffrey, the rumbustious Wilson were long since dead, Jeffrey in 1850, Wilson in the same year as Lockhart. The gentle and beloved Dean Ramsay had departed, full of years, in 1872.

There were genial ghosts and good memories, and she recalled them with a happy wistfulness in what was probably the last article she wrote; 'Reminiscences of Edinburgh Nearly Fifty Years Ago', for *Longman's Magazine* in January 1893. This is one of the sources—along with her contemporary Journal—for our knowledge of her life in Edinburgh, before her marriage. It is full of the grace of old age, with none of its acerbity, self-pity, or garrulity; a tantalizing fragment of what might have been a most entertaining autobiography had she chosen to write that, as crown of her work.

It had been preceded by another chapter of memories—in June, 1892: *Reminiscences of St. Petersburg.* She saw both cities, so different in atmosphere and society, with the clarity that age brings to the remembrance of youth and early middle age.

These Reminiscences recalled her second visit to Russia in 1844, when she was already the author of *Letters From the Shores of the Baltic*, a contributor to *The Quarterly*, a personage in the society of both Edinburgh and London. She had been accompanied by her maid Anderson, in some degree a chaperon and companion as well as help, who had been extremely indignant at the impertinence of Customs officials in searching her lady's wardrobe.

As on her first visit to St. Petersburg, Elizabeth had gone first to Mrs. Wilson's English boarding-house, then to private hosts. She was lavishly entertained. At the Opera she saw the Empress who had a passion for dress—her one solace for being palsied at forty. Under her gorgeous gowns she was said to be encased in flannel. On this occasion she was ablaze with diamonds; and half-way through the performance, while Taglioni danced on the stage. Her Majesty withdrew into a dressing-room behind the Imperial Box, to reappear in a new gown with even more diamonds.

Elizabeth recalled one of the famous masked balls at Court. Only the women wore masks, and they were allowed considerable freedom. They might even flirt with the Emperor. For a frolic, Elizabeth and a Russian friend of equal height agreed to dress alike in black domino; she found herself involved in a succession of 'signs, taps, shakes of the hand and offers of the arm'. She promptly made up to a young count whom she had met in London, teased and quizzed him unmercifully, and finally informed him that he 'was both *enlaidi* and *engraissé*,' then 'threw him over'. There followed a slight comedy of mistaken identity: one 'little, pert-looking officer', mistaking her for her Russian double, teased her about having large feet.

'I prided myself not a little on my feet'—which were, apparently, not large—reflected the old lady complacently; so she displayed them in their elegant black satin sandals, to the confusion of the pert one.

Another asked if she spoke English, and was told: 'A leetle', which induced him to converse in French and to pronounce the English '*le peuple le plus detestable au monde*'. This was not to be borne; it 'would have been too much for a saint, so I broke out: "No, sir, I beg your pardon; the noblest, the freest, you know what I mean—the freest, in the world"'. The critic left her hastily, doubtless registering in his mind as dangerous this 'tall woman in a black domino and with a small foot, who endeavoured to incite the lieges against the Government'.

Yet another partner recognized her as English because she said: '*Oh oui*' and '*Oh non*' and 'only the English use the interjection "Oh" in everything'.

It was fun, but on the whole she disliked those balls: 'A masquerade of only women is, for the most part, deficient in go and repartee. The women may be divided into three heads—the shy, the bold, and the stupid. The shy say timid things, the bold rude things, aad the stupid say nothing at all.' At the hair-brushing that night Anderson stated rather than asked: 'You will never go to that place again'; to which her mistress meekly agreed: 'No, never.'

All the same, it was good to remember, forty years on and more, as were the parties in Edinburgh including another, livelier masquerade. The old lady recalled it all with affection. She was living a good deal in the past, and most of it was sunlit, not a place of shadows.

An old friend, Mrs. Boyle, afterwards described having tea with her in Fitzroy Square. The room was full of pictures, many of them Sir Charles's own; the portrait of him by Opie; a treasured Bellini. There was, too, a bust of the Queen. The desk was covered with papers. The old lady sat by the tea-table, pouring out first of all a saucer of milk for the little grey cat.

She was always interesting because herself so interested in people, books and things, never bored, always serene and very kind. But she could be 'grandly out-spoken' about cruelty, injustice, cowardice. Her health was good; she used to attribute that to eating apples, and John the Third used to send her Ribstone Pippins from his garden at Wimbledon.[1] In the last year or

---

[1] John Murray the Third died 1892.

two she admitted to being 'addicted to recumbency', but never to any lethargy of mind. 'My time passes quietly, but it is no misfortune to be thrown on books, and I can even read dull ones if they are interesting—which sounds rather Irish'—but is completely clear to any book-lover.

She was of those who always turn to books, for entertainment and companionship as well as for instruction, who find it on the whole easier to read than to abstain from reading. There were friends too; not many, now, of her own generation, but younger folk came and were kind and welcome. And memories were a thronging company. She had seen most of the century, and the reign, from Coronation to Jubilee and beyond, of the beloved Queen, her junior by ten years, whose widowhood she had, by her words, helped to solace.

Her memory went back to England of the Regency, just emerging from the long shadow of war and fear of invasion, recalling, perhaps, the bonfires and the lighting of candles in the windows for the victory of Waterloo. She could remember the death of the poor, mad old King, the reigns of his two sons, the brilliant and raffish George, the amiable, slight-witted William; the spell cast by the young Queen in her youth and virtue.

In memory she saw her childhood again, in Norwich and Framlingham, all the freedom and country pleasures in which her sensible mother indulged her and her sisters and brothers; the change of life in Germany, with new customs, new interests, new studies; the awakening of the impulse to write. Then came her sister's marriage and departure, the long separation; the invitation to visit the strange country of her adoption, the stormy voyage, the long journey across snowy plains, the strange inns, the home-coming to that beloved sister and her children; all the new way of life in dear, familiar company, the crowding upon her mind of new pictures, impressions, acquaintances; the increasing urge to write. She could feel again the thrill of acceptance, of seeing herself in print; the warmth of admiration offered her by John Murray and dear Lockhart. This had been the be-

Mrs. Alexander Smith, mother-in-law of John Murray III,
by Elizabeth Rigby 1844

ginning of more than a chapter in her life, or of a chapter that continued almost to the end of the story, along with the domestic narrative that was so full and rich. Indeed that chapter was only now ended, the last words written, the last proofs corrected.

Her career, so new, almost daring at the time, had brought both work and friendships, and these of a subtly different quality from what she would have made as simply a woman at home, or the wife of her husband. Dearest of all was Lockhart: she saw him so vividly, with his proud head and dark sad eyes, the small mouth that could sneer as well as smile, the manner that was so aloof to some, but to her always so warm, so kind, so humorous.

She remembered her first meeting with Charles Eastlake at John Murray's dinner-table: that gentle courtesy, that mutual sympathy so quickly realized, the growth of friendship, the new warmth and wonder, the fulfilment in marriage, the years of true companionship. These years made a brilliant pageant of memories: the parties where people looked at her and whispered about her admiringly; the splendid rooms, banked with flowers; a beautiful duchess, with head wreathed in diamonds, coming gracefully to greet her; the Queen, still young and radiant, and of incomparable dignity, dancing the quadrille, then making her solitary and queenly way back to her throne.

Again she travelled those happy journeys—to Venice, the beloved enchantress, to so many famed cities; all the fun, the discoveries came back to her, the richness of art, the beauty, above all the dear companionship. Then came the shadowed way on which she must walk alone towards acceptance and faith.

The sunshine and the darkness alike lay behind her now. The path was a twilit one, very level, not hard to follow, with no long prospect, very peaceful.

'Time is relentless; I feel myself nearing the goal,' she wrote, at the beginning of 1892, 'without fear, I may thankfully say.'

As her time drew near she begged:

'Pray for my release. I have had more blessings and what is called success than most people; I have also drunk to the bottom of a very bitter cup, for which, perhaps, I ought to be thankful. At all events, it is a mercy to be weaned from life when one is about to leave it.'

She died on the 2nd of October, 1893, almost at the end of her eighty-fourth year: a pioneer in the now flourishing and changing craft of journalism; a woman of great vigour of mind and character. She was not always gentle. Her strong prejudices, her outspoken opinions, her uninhibited pungency of expression made her a formidable adversary. There have been many more amiable women, as well as many inspired by that creative genius to which she could never lay claim; but in her large and colourful personality she is one to be remembered and enjoyed. If she does not lead the procession of eminent Victorian women, she still holds her place.

BIBLIOGRAPHY

Eastlake, Sir Charles. *Contribution to the Literature of the Fine Arts Series 2 with memoir by Lady Eastlake.* John Murray, 1870

Eastlake, Lady. *Fellowship: Letters to my Sister Mourners.* Macmillan, 1868

Eastlake, Lady. *Letters from the Shores of the Baltic.* John Murray, 1844

Eastlake, Lady. *Journals and Correspondence.* Edited by Charles Eastlake Smith. John Murray, 1895

James, Admiral Sir William. *The Order of Release.* John Murray, 1947

Lochhead, Marion. *John Gibson Lockhart.* John Murray, 1954

Longman's Magazine: June, 1892, January, 1893

Murray's Magazine: September 1891

Paston, George. *At John Murray's.* John Murray, 1932

Quarterly Review, The, 1841–1891. Vols. 64–172.

Smiles, Samuel. *A Publisher and His Friends.* John Murray, 1891

Unpublished letters of Lady Eastlake to John Murray II and III.

INDEX